I0117799

Beyond the Crooked Bridge

An Adventurous Life throughout Idaho

First Edition

Eloise E. Kraemer

DEDICATION

I thought when I completed my original book, "Across the Crooked Bridge", that I said all I had to say. Slowly, I began to realize that my whole life is entwined in the story I feel compelled to tell.

In this book, I attempt to give you a view of this great state's past and present through the eyes of lifelong residents who have continued to lead an adventurous life while learning to love and appreciate every corner of Idaho.

I feel that the simpler the first course of a meal is, the greater you appreciate each course thereafter. Learning about new places, meeting new people and learning about the history behind a town or a state can be as enjoyable as an evening at a concert with good friends and a fine meal afterwards.

I hope you will enjoy a taste of these adventures and be stirred to visit some of the locations described in this book.

I dedicate this book to all who consider themselves 'Children of Idaho', young or old. Keep reaching, be curious, ask questions and continue learning.

FORWARD

I begin this writing less than a mile from the spot where I ended the earlier book. I ended the book at the west end of the Silver Valley where I captured a picture of a moose serenely grazing at the water's edge.

I sat watching a flock of geese flying overhead, calling to their leader, while he worked his way northwest, returning to prime nesting grounds. A pair of wood ducks was anxiously guarding their new summer digs while a lone egret called anxiously to her mate, who was winging his way home, with dinner.

I knew two things as I sat quietly, taking in the scene that spring morning. First, I needed to write a book about my love for this Valley and what it meant to grow up here. Secondly, I knew that it was time, after over 45 years, to return home.

I now sit at my desk in our newly built home, in a forest, upon a hill, overlooking the waters where I watched that moose. A fire is glowing in the wood stove, my own dogs, not my sister's, are snoozing contentedly at my feet. The cat dozes in the rocker. A full moon shines overhead through clouds racing across the sky, chased by an autumn wind, rushing to push the colors of fall towards a snow filled world, blanketing the trees and fields with a white cover until spring. I am ready for the transformation. I am excited about the change of seasons, just as I am excited about a new day. I always look forward to the first shoots of new flowers pushing their way through the wet soil in the spring, the drying grasses and warm breezes of summer, the first falling leaves with all their bright colors in the fall and the first snow, big lazy flakes, soft and cold on my face in the winter!

I love seasons! This afternoon I told the dogs, "I feel change in the air".

The cat leaped of the couch, and slid across the floor. She did a side-flip and hopped up on one of the kitchen chairs, twitching her tail, as if to say, "Yep...I feel it too!"

The dogs figured it meant that I was taking them out for a walk and all ran for the door with a series of barks.

"Okay, you win....but, when I get back, I start my book. I am going to write that book I said I wouldn't. If you keep clear of rolling in deer or elk poop, I might just let you be in the book."

"Let's go take that walk, now."

They must have understood, because they still smell acceptable, so, now, I can get started.

1

When the Comet Hit

At 18 years of age, I thought I had my life all planned out. I had a job I enjoyed working at a newspaper in Wallace, Idaho, the same town I was born and raised in and never wanted to leave.

I began the job in hopes of saving enough to go to nursing school for four years. I was now a full year in to it, and was starting to build a savings account, but also was realizing that I might have to pare down expectations and go for a local practical nursing course.

One Friday, in late May I prepared to go out on a date after work with a young man I had been dating for about seven months. We had a lot in common and never ran out of things to talk about. I could already call him a "best friend".

When he picked me up at my house he told me that we would be going to the restaurant along Lake Coeur d'Alene that we loved called the "Shady Rest". As we passed between Pinehurst and Cataldo on the old highway, which was two lane, and wound past farm fields, an old gentleman was working in his field by the highway. He raised his hand and waved as we cruised by in a red and white 1960 Chevrolet (the kind with tail fins). I remember thinking what a beautiful day it had been as the sun was getting lower in the sky. It was a perfect spring day and I was looking forward to a perfect evening by the lake.

In those days, US 10 wound along Coeur d'Alene Lake from the east, crossing Blue Creek Bay Bridge and heading into Coeur d'Alene. The Shady Rest restaurant was located to the north of the bridge with a beautiful view of the lake.

The radio was playing, and I was busy talking about my plans for going to my girlfriend's graduation that coming weekend. We wore no seatbelts back then. Back in 1967, girls on dates usually scooted over beside the driver so that they could operate the radio better, I think. Anyway, that was where I was.

Then, in just one moment, in just one blink of time. Everything changed.

A comet shot out of the sky; a 3600 pound steel comet, black and white, with tail fins. Of course, a comet has to have tail fins! It crossed the yellow divider line painted on the same piece of asphalt we were traveling on and collided head on with our red and white 3600 pound steel comet, of course, with tail fins.

What are the odds? Here were two 3600 pound steel 1960 Chevys, identical except for color. Each vehicle was traveling at approximately 60 miles per hour in the opposite direction, one black, one white, meeting and wanting to occupy the same exact space at the same exact moment in time?

I read somewhere that he following happens when comets collide in space: "When large objects impact terrestrial planets such as the Earth, there can be significant physical and biospherical consequences".

Well, that is just how I can explain the effect of what hit me. It is said that a shooting star or falling star, is the visible passage of a comet or asteroid, or meteoroid through Earth's atmosphere, after being heated to incandescence by collisions with air molecules in the upper atmosphere, creating a streak of light via its rapid motion

That's all I remember, just a streak of light and......nothing.

The thing that saved me from going through that window, I believe, to this day, is that my boyfriend was used to taking his little niece and nephew with him in the car. Back in 1967, you could throw as many kids as you wanted in the front seat with you, so you could keep your eye on them. They either sat or stood on the seat while you drove. If you had to put your brakes on fast, you just threw your arm out and caught them.

My boyfriend had become quite adept at throwing his arm out to catch a wayward niece or nephew. When I came sailing forward, he put his arm out. I ended up with a bruise across my chest, but I am certain it saved my life. In turn, he ended up with a deep bruise, causing a lump on his arm that, to my knowledge, has never gone away.

The first thing I saw was impossible. I saw people working on me to extricate my right leg and check my head that had been implanted in the front window. I was looking down on all of them while they worked. It was interesting.

That was my only cloudy thought. Just one muddled thought, "interesting".

My second cloudy awakening was seeing who I thought was god. He looked down on me with worried beautiful sky blue eyes. Oh, maybe it wasn't God after all. Maybe it was just the guy in the ambulance. What beautiful eyes.

Ouch! I woke for a moment once again and I was on a table where they just finished stitching up my leg. It had a long gash that ran the length from a mashed ankle with a severed tendon to about half way up to the knee in a crooked path. I felt nothing except for that last stitch. My waking lasted about one second and all went black.

The next morning I was awakened when my mother, father and boyfriend arrived in the room. To this day, I do not remember any nurses, just the doctor talking to my parents. I do not remember a face on the doctor, which is too bad, because when I returned many months later to thank him, I found that he left right after tending to me to go on a fishing trip in Alaska. His plane crashed and he was killed. I never got to thank him.

That morning, although I was still in a haze, I was able to convince the doctor that I was well enough to go home. I don't think they took as many x-rays back then of heads or necks, or maybe we were just expected to not break as easy, because I had no x-rays taken, to my knowledge.

I finally made it home, after losing anything I had in my stomach at least three separate times on the way. That was not something that was foreign to my parents, however. The road home was curvy, and all my life I suffered with bouts of car-sickness. They probably thought it was not too far out of line.

When I got home, they found it was not going to be that

easy for me to go to bed in my bedroom upstairs. I would have to navigate a number of stairs to go to the bathroom and the only way would be to crawl. My leg and ankle were not ready to walk yet. To add to the problem, getting up or moving around upset my stomach.

I camped on the couch.

Now, you have to understand that my family consisted of nine people. Fortunately, my older sister was now married and my older brother was in college in Spokane, Washington. The family entertainment room was the living room, which was also where the television and couch were.

That evening, the kids turned on the television. The lights flashed, the noise was deafening. No matter how low they turned the television, it was excruciating. No matter how I turned and hid my head, I saw lights flashing. My head hurt. It pounded, I pressed and the pressure pressed back. It felt like my head was going to explode. I threw up. My mother made the kids shut off the television. They complained. I screamed. Everyone went to bed. I slept and moaned.

This went on for three days. I could not keep food down. I needed help going to the bathroom and back, or I crawled. On the third day, my father loaded me in the car and took me to the local hospital in Wallace, the Providence Hospital.

I loved that hospital. I was a candy-striper (volunteer nursing assistant) at the hospital when I was in high school. The Catholic sister's that ran the hospital spoiled us. They would let us get desserts out of the fridge on our breaks. We helped a lot, too. We learned to take blood pressure and temperature readings, make beds and give simple sponge baths to the female patients, or just read to young children. The worst part was emptying bed pans. The scariest part was when they would have us go alone down to the dungeon-like basement to get something. It was dark and cold. There were ancient incubators and old steel cribs and old x-ray machines from probably the 1930s or 1940s. It was pretty spooky.

I don't remember much other than them putting me to bed in the hospital. I went to sleep and didn't want to wake up. I don't know how many days I slept, but I remember people coming in and trying to wake me to see me over the days. I remember they always asked how my leg was and I always said it was fine, I didn't feel it at all because my head hurt too much. When they left I was happy to just go back to sleep so my head didn't hurt. I remember my boyfriend came and left me with a little fuzzy stuffed dog. It stayed by my side and helped me sleep. That was good because all I wanted to do was sleep.

One day one of the head nurses, a sister, came in and insisted I wake. I remember I didn't want to. She told me I had to try harder to stay awake or I was going to go to sleep and never wake. Then she told me of a lady that went to sleep after a concussion and never woke for years. When she woke she found she had slept her whole life and was now an old lady with gray hair. That scared me. I tried a little harder to stay awake, but my head still hurt.

2

Another Me

I started having dreams more. Then, sometimes I started wondering if I was dreaming or awake. It seems like sometimes I was inside myself, and other times I could go outside myself and see how other people saw things. I decided to experiment with this.

I was now to the point where I was exercising my leg daily, getting up and walking down the hall and back to my room. I liked to go down the hall to the room where they kept the newborn babies. I could look in the window at them. They all looked so cute and cuddly all swaddled up in their little blankets, sleeping, making little faces like they just had a bad dream, or squirming and fussing as they got hungry.

A sister walked up to me and asked if I liked babies. All of a sudden, I decided to see how she would react if I told her something shocking. I said, "Oh yes, they are so cute! Why, they look almost good enough to eat!"

Now, to this day, I have no idea what came over me. But, at the time, I can remember feeling a sort of uncanny glee as I saw the horror on her face. She bustled away into the back kitchen area across the hall where they had a sort of break room for the nurses.

I heard muted conversations. A few minutes later, a nurse came out and suggested it was time I return to my room. After that, they kept a close eye on me. I made no further outlandish comments.

I think a part of my brain did become irreparably damaged. In the process, I think another part of my brain took over or woke up. I think there are many perspectives to anything and I probably began to spend more time trying to understand situations from more than one perspective.

It took the summer for my head to stop hurting so violently. I finally returned to work in August when school was ready to start. I had a new outlook on life. Life is too short and to important not to try to make a difference. I needed to not just mark time in life. I needed to make a difference.

I started to question myself and became more curious about the world around me. I became actually adventurous and curious about what lay beyond the small town and Valley I grew up in. I made more frequent trips to Spokane, Washington on the weekends, many times with my younger sister, or my best friend, Mary for companionship.

I still dated my old boyfriend, but things changed. It was like everything on earth shifted a couple of degrees. I still looked like the same person when I looked in the mirror, but I felt like someone else was inside me questioning things I never even considered before. When I would disagree, or question things that I never questioned before, he didn't understand why I changed.

Many times, especially if the weather would change, my head would begin to ache violently. This made me short tempered and changeable. I realize, now that it must have been very hard for him to understand my changing moods.

We fought. We never fought, before. It was hard for both of us to understand. We broke up that summer, to just get back together again in the fall, but it was never the same. We eventually broke up for good.

He has always been and will always be a good person and lifelong friend.

My best friend, Mary and her mother took art classes in oil painting at the Kellogg YMCA. I joined them and learned I loved to oil paint. I also started bowling. That winter, I learned to ski and started going skiing regularly every weekend with my girlfriend. Life was opening up!

Between work and these activities I kept busy. It isn't

that easy to date in a small town where most of the young people your age are either working in the mines and already married, going to college or in the service. (This was during the Vietnam War period).

I did date a couple of guys for very short periods. I remember one kid my brother brought home with him that was attending Spokane Community College. They both received degrees as electronic technicians and were leaving that coming Monday to report to basic training in the Air Force. He was a farm boy from Rockford, Washington. He asked if I wanted to go to the movies in town with him. I thought that would be nice, so we loaded up in my car and drove to the movies. When we got there, he confessed that he didn't have a dime on him. Ha ha...good thing I brought my purse.

At work, I couldn't have asked for a better supervisor, R.J. Bruning, editor of the North Idaho Press in Wallace. He was patient when I was learning to be a teletype-setter. Basically, I typed all the regular print for articles in the paper. This was before offset printing. All newspaper articles were typed by a machine that created a punch tape. The tape punched out a code in paper tape (two dots above for a, dot on top two on bottom for b, etc...I got so I could read it easily). While you typed, you learned how to easily figure how many n and m spaces to put in a line to make the type line up for the columns. Today, this is all done automatically. The tape was then put into a large linotype machine in the back of the newspaper office. As the tape was read by the machine, it dropped the letters onto a plate. Hot lead was poured over the letters. After the lines of letters cool, the lead blocks were arranged on a tray, making up the newspaper page in lead letters. Richard, the man who operated the linotype machine, printed out the larger lettered headlines and newspaper add headings directly on the machine keyboard in much the same way. The difference was that when he typed, each key would send a metal letter down to be formed in lead. When all the page trays were ready, (basically laid out like a newspaper in lead), it was loaded into a large printing press with enormous rollers that fed out sheets of newspaper. Those sheets ran over the inked sheets of lead pressing a print copy of ink on the paper.

Now everything is done with photo offset printing. Soon, even offset printing will be part of the past. Your newspapers will all be only online.

The editor let my co-workers in the front office show me how to proofread so that I could fill in during the absence of our regular proofreader. I learned yet another skill.

Then, one day the editor decided to see how my photographic skills were. He was attending an evening meeting, but was also supposed to be taking pictures of a local talent show. He showed me how to operate the press camera and sent me.

Hey! That was fun! My pictures turned out decent enough that occasionally I was asked to take pictures and report for him after that. I really enjoyed taking the pictures.

The editor was gaining confidence in me. I loved reading his editorials, and really looked up to him, so it made me feel pretty good about myself. Sometimes he needed to attend meetings early in the afternoon. He approached me and asked if I would like to "finish the front page of the paper". This was better than if he offered me a day off! He asked me pick appropriate articles off the Associated Press teletype and type them up to fill in any extra spaces in the front page of the paper.

After I successfully completed this mission, I was frequently asked to do this. I had now learned yet another part to creating a daily paper!

The fall that I turned 21 years old, I started dating a local school teacher. Doug also grew up in Wallace, but was older. Although I had seen him around town, we had never met.

I first met Doug in my senior year. Doug only had his

student teaching to complete to get his teaching certificate. He completed his student teaching the first semester, teaching chemistry, advanced math, print and photo and physics. The teacher that was supposed to be teaching fell ill, so Doug was hired to continue teaching for the rest of the year.

I hadn't seen Doug, or Mr. Kraemer, as I referred to him, since the last day of my senior year. Then, there he was one day in the newspaper office. I was busy typing up the paper. Doug and his best friend stopped in to see the editor, his best friend's father. Doug came through the back office that day and paused by my desk to ask where the bathroom was. As I told him, he got a strange look on his face and asked if he knew me from somewhere. I told him, yes, he taught me my senior year in Chemistry. He smiled and said something like, "Oh, hi."

As he turned, he slammed his face into the corner of the door casing. Ouch! I tried not to laugh as I hid my face.

A couple of weeks later, I needed a ride home. The editor's son and Doug offered to take me. As we crossed the crooked bridge, Doug made the statement, "Man, no one could get ME to drive across this!"

Now, there was a challenge.

That fall, Doug called and asked me out.

About that time, I decided that it was taking too long to save up enough money to go to nursing school. I came up with an alternate plan.

I really admired our family dentist, Dr. Rice. Insurance wasn't something that many employers provided for employees in my early years. It wasn't until I was in the ninth grade in school before dental insurance was available to the miners and mill workers where my father worked. By the time that became available, I was already pretty frightened of dentists. My only experience with them was to get bad molars yanked out of my mouth.

Dr. Rice came up with an affordable plan to fix any problem teeth on all of the children left at home at that time. The plan that was affordable for my parents with the dental insurance that was awarded with my father's new pay package.

Dr. Rice was kind and gentle. He took x-rays, a new experience. He used a numbing compound to rub on your gums so you didn't feel the pain of the injection while his caring assistants assured us that our fears were unfounded.

The last time I went in for a checkup, I asked the dental

assistant what she did to learn how to become an assistant. She explained that she apprenticed with the doctor.

I used to go to lunch at a lunch counter across the street from the North Idaho Press, which was located on Cedar Street in Wallace. The lunch counter was in Morrow's Department store, which is now the Brooks Hotel.

Many times, sitting at the counter, eating my lunch, I noticed Dr. Rice a little ways down the lunch counter, having his lunch.

I decided to offer him a proposition.

I approached him one afternoon while he was eating his lunch. I asked him if he would consider taking me on as an apprentice dental assistant. I told him I would work for free at first until he was satisfied with my work.

Even though I made a whole $2.50 an hour at the North Idaho Press, which was not bad money in those days, I owned my car outright, and lived at home. I did buy groceries as a way to pay rent, and bought my own clothes, but that was not talking that much money. I had money in savings for school. I would just use that.

He said he would consider it, and let me know.

A few weeks later, Dr. Rice called me and asked me to

come in for an interview. After the interview, he hired me. He even said he would pay me $1.35 an hour for my apprenticeship, which he set at 3 months. After that time, I would be reviewed.

I was never so happy or proud! I loved dental assisting! I was learning and helping people! They also did their own dental lab work in the back. I learned how to make gold crowns.

I had no idea how many ways my new skills would come in handy throughout my life.

3

A Beginning at the End or the Beginning

I begin this chapter at the end of my life in the Silver Valley (for many years), and at the beginning of my new life.

This also happened to be on one of the last days of the 1960s and the beginning of a new decade, the 1970s.

It also happened to be the day I was wed.

I dated my husband, Doug, for only three months, but we knew something of each other for over three years. I knew of his existence all my life. He also grew up in the small town of Wallace, Idaho.

He came from a different background than I. He was raised as an only child, and in "town" in a neighborhood. His father was a banker.

In comparison, I was raised in a family of seven children, in the country, (mountainous country). My father was a worked in a mill as a flotation operator in the mining industry. He also worked side jobs. He had a company called "Kite Mining Company". He tore down and cleaned up old mill sites.

Doug and I are opposite in our way of thinking and solving problems, yet our end goal and purpose usually aligns. Early on, this fact intrigued and frustrated the both of us. However, this fact has worked well throughout our marriage in solving problems. We can pretty much come at any problem from two sides.

In a small town in a small state in the late 1960s, the choice to marry seemed like a good one. Doug was my best friend. I was twenty-one and still hadn't saved enough money to go to college. Doug was leaving to go to the other end of the state for a job and a long winter loomed ahead.

I decided it would be a good idea to get married and a sign of true love if I went with him to the other end of the state to see if we could survive on the income of an Idaho State Patrolman.

In the late 1960s and early 1970s, the income for an Idaho State Patrolman was below welfare level if you were married. No, we did not collect welfare. We just lived on a mighty thin budget, as did all of the young patrolmen. I planned to continue dental assisting, but early on in the marriage, Doug made it clear that he did not care for me working outside the home. That would change with time.

I really didn't decide to marry him all that fast.

The first time he told me he was going to quit his teaching job and join the Idaho State Police, I decided I was going to stop going out with him. Who wanted to go out with a policeman? He would probably arrest me if I drove too fast!

I never got around to refusing a date, however. Our dates were always filled with unexpected outcomes and adventure. We would follow roads up into the mountains that came out in all sorts of places I had never explored. I guess Doug just kind of "grew" on me. I guess you could say that our dates were happy and comfortable, like spending time with a friend.

When we first started dating, we would have times when we both were rather quiet, not knowing just how to get a conversation started. Doug invented comical friend called Cletus Cluckenclacker.

Now, I knew from the first that Cletus was fictitious, but he was a great conversation piece. We just kept building on the scenario. Cletus became a fast friend and got us through some tough times.

He was a rather rotund long-haul truck driver. He had some unusual problems, such as having an uncanny love of any kind of candy bar and not being able to read road maps very well. Once he got lost on an old logging road with his triple trailer rig and was forced to live on his truck load of candy bars until they finally discovered his location and brought in a helicopter to air-lift the tractor and trailers to the main highway.

Cletus gained so much weight from the candy bars that a separate helicopter was brought in to airlift him out. The poor guy got air sick, however, so, in the end, poor Cletus had to be brought out on a mule.

That caused some new problems when it was discovered that Cletus was allergic to mules.

 I am sorry to say that Cletus ended up with a bad case of hives. His boss, being the kind sort, took pity on him and sent him to Hawaii to recover.

Well, enough of Cletus Cluckenclacker. Surprisingly, to this day, if my husband and I go through a rough patch, one of us will bring up Cletus and happen to "remember" some scenario where Cletus and his family had it much worse.

We got married, (my husband, Doug...NOT Cletus...and I), December 19, 1969 and left that day to our new home in Kamiah, Idaho, where he was to start his new career as an Idaho State Policeman as a Weigh Master at a weigh station for trucks over 16,000 pounds traveling the State highways.

In those days, all Idaho State Patrolmen began their

careers as weigh masters, and eventually were promoted to patrolmen.

So my husband, with a Bachelor of Science degree in Chemistry and Physics from the University of Idaho, and teacher's certificate for the State of Idaho, became an Idaho State Patrolman recruit.

I said he was crazy, but he said he wanted some adventure and wanted to establish "his own identity". He also said he wanted to help people, and thought this was a good way to accomplish both. He was interested in putting his physics background to work in accident investigation.

I was excited to start an adventure like they have in romance novels like one I remember reading called "Mrs. Mike", where a lady from New York married a Royal Canadian Mounted Policeman and moved to the Yukon.

4

Leaving the Silver Valley

As we left the Silver Valley on the day of our marriage, we traveled through Wallace's neighboring town to the west, Osburn. This roughly eight mile section of the I-90 freeway, (west of Silverton, and east of Kellogg, Idaho), had just opened. I-90 runs from coast to coast across the United States.   The Osburn section was the fourth section of freeway across the Idaho Panhandle to be built, leaving only two more to go to complete the total freeway build from the west to the east coast across the United States. The two sections left were west Silverton, Idaho to east Wallace, Idaho, (a total 2.5 mile section) and the Lookout Pass section, east of Mullan to the Montana border (a six mile section).

Big changes were about to take place in our corner of the world and we were leaving.

A light snow was beginning to fall as we headed for a two night stay in Spokane, Washington before turning south to our new home in Kamiah, Idaho.

As we drove along, I began thinking back to my family's beginnings in the Silver Valley. My thoughts were spurred on by the conversation that Doug and I were having in the car about our new life we were about to begin and the new section of freeway we were driving over which buried some past history to make room for progress and a new layer of history.

The two very first sections of I-90 to impact our world, were the east Wallace to west Mullan, Idaho section, and the Fourth of July Pass Section. Both took place in the early 1960s.

The Wallace to Mullan section of I-90 was the first highway built in Idaho to cost $1,000,000 a mile. The South fork of the Coeur d'Alene River, a major highway, a railroad, and in three places, an interchange and access road needed to be squeezed between two mountains less than 200 feet wide in places. Some old landmarks disappeared as a result, such as Clarks Store and Cabins, on the eastern edge of Wallace, and some ancient log cabins owned by Amel and Isabelle Hurdy, on the south side of the road in the Golconda District.

My mother's sister, husband and child and my father's brother and his wife, all lived in the cabins across from the Golconda back in the late 1930s. My grandfather came down from Sandpoint, Idaho to also work in the mines. He was staying with his daughter and son-in-law. My grandfather incurred an unfortunate accident at the mine and injured his leg. My grandmother sent my mother, who was 16 at the time, to help care for him.

Her sister was pregnant. She already had her hands full with their young son. Needless to say, my mother met my father. He chased her for the next four years before she let him put a ring on her finger.

The Golconda District at exit 64 is the site of the old Golconda Mill, (you can still see marks on the mountain on the north side of the highway about even with the overpass bridge), The Golconda mill closed in the spring of 1960 after the opening of the Lucky Friday Mill on the site of the Lucky Friday mine, which was already in production, in Mullan, Idaho.

The Lucky Friday Mill began its operation in February of 1960. The Golconda Mill was, thereafter, placed on a standby basis until its demise in 1975.

A freeway exit, which was already in the freeway plans, was built and named the "Golconda Exit" at Exit 64. It still remains.

The new freeway obscured a large section of the original Mullan Trail but took out a dangerous curve in the old road design, famously called "Dead Man's Curve". The curve claimed numerous lives of Valley residents over the years.

Snow was sticking on Fourth of July Pass as we neared the top. Fog was settling in. I felt it was an ominous warning that if we continued on, we could never again return to the Silver Valley.

At the summit of Fourth of July Canyon, I could just glimpse the mouth of the old tunnel, part of the old highway to the north of the divided highway were driving on. The original Mullan Road veered off to the north of the present highway. A tunnel was made through the mountains in the 1920s. It remained part of the highway until 1957 when the road over the pass was widened into a divided highway, yet, not a freeway. The highway was moved a bit to the south and the summit lowered somewhat.

I can still remember riding in a car as a child in the 1950s through the tunnel. Dad would always turn the lights on. Doug and I laughed, sharing memories, because both parents, (and probably many more from the Valley), would beep the horn as they went through the tunnel. It wasn't actually required, but was fun and echoed eerily. It always made me feel better, because, by that time, on the mountain roads, as a child, I would be feeling pretty car sick.

The tunnel peered out at me in the distance through the driving snow. "Don't gooo00," it seemed to say. "Unknown waters lie ahead. You will get lost in the mist and never return."

I turned on the radio. The Beatles were playing on the radio. I decided to think about the future and close the door on the past.

Little did I know how long it would be before I could once again call the Silver Valley my home.

5

South of the Valley

Our first home was in a trailer park by the Middle Fork of the Clearwater River on the outskirts of Kamiah, Idaho. I immediately fell in love with our newly adopted home town. It was and still is very small, but extremely friendly.

Our home consisted of an 8 foot by 32 foot yellow and white 1950s mobile home...No...it was a trailer. It came complete with pink toilet and bathtub. The trailer consisted of a small bedroom with single bed to the back, a walk through bathroom, a combo kitchen and dining area and a grand living room complete with front door facing the wind side. That part would have been great for air conditioning in the summer. The problem was that the temperatures that December were unusually cold. Things were pretty cool when we moved in on the twenty-first of December.

We fired up the oil pot burner, kept our coats on and proceeded to make it our home. Doug needed to go to work the next day and worked right up until Christmas Eve. He got Christmas Eve and Christmas off.

We were determined to start our very own life, so, even though both parents asked us to come home for

Christmas, and we could have driven up and back in a day, we elected to have our first Christmas by ourselves.

The day before Christmas we walked to town together. I swear it was warmer outside than in our little tin box house. We agreed that we could afford a whopping five dollars each to purchase Christmas gifts for each other. Gifts were given to family members before we left home.

We took our five dollars and went opposite ways, each choosing a side of the street. I believe the town contained just two places worth shopping for a five dollar gift in. On one side of the street was the local hardware. On the other side was a gift shop. I took the gift shop, Doug took the hardware. Doug presented me with a corning ware cake dish. I presented Doug with a metal box. Inside was a cap pistol.

The Idaho State Police didn't issue side arms to weigh masters. I figured he should have some sort of protection in that little weigh-station, just in case. Backup from a full-fledged State Patrolman could take a good deal of time.

Thankfully, he never needed to use his cap pistol. He got along pretty good with the local loggers.

We drove up to see the newly constructed Dworshak Dam above Orofino, Idaho on Christmas Day. Construction had just started. It was an awesome sight. At a height of 717 feet, it is the third tallest dam in the

United States and the tallest straight-axis concrete dam in the Western Hemisphere. Construction began in 1966 and the dam was completed in 1973. It was and still is the only lake on the Clearwater River.

Our education on Idaho outside of the Silver Valley and other facts of life was beginning.

6

The Castle

It took us only a month and a half to decide that love and a pot burning oil stove was not enough to keep us warm for the remainder of the winter. Even if we could put on enough layers of clothes to keep us warm, there remained the fact that the cans of food in the shelves were actually freezing at night.

We went shopping one evening. When I awoke and opened the cupboard. The next morning, I found all the cans frozen on the shelf!

The day that really took the cake was the day that Doug left for work at his little weigh station (box about the size of an 8x10 shed) with an awesome electric heater in it.

I sat at home trying to write a letter with gloves on. My feet were freezing in boots. I got up and tapped the thermostat. The pot burner stove was going like real Hell probably looks. The little thermometer on the kitchen cabinet read, but I couldn't believe it. Yep, it was correct. It read thirty-two, 32, degrees! Doug got a phone call.

That evening we took our usual walk around the trailer

park and past the brand new 12x64 trailers, "Four Seasons" brands, and the awesome "Marlette" (Cadillac of the new mobile home craze). We took a quick stroll through the more practical, less pricy, Four Season trailer. What a dream! Doug mentioned that a lot of State Policemen were choosing trailers for their permanent homes.

When the State Police transferred a patrolman from one duty station to another, the state paid their moves if it was a promotion. If the policeman owned a mobile home, the State would pay to move it in lieu of moving furniture separately. It made sense.

A few days later our new Four Seasons 12x64, three bedroom, one and a half bath trailer, with furniture and beautiful avocado green shag carpet was sitting on its own lot. We were homeowners! We made a down payment on our new $7,000 home and paid $72 a month payments. We owned our own home! It felt like a true castle! No cans froze that night. I felt like I was in heaven!

7

Puff, the Cat and Lewiston, Idaho

I really missed our family's dog, left back at home with my parents, sisters and little brother.

Married life was one great adventure. It had its drawbacks. The first big surprise was that I expected to get a job as a dental assistant or maybe in a local newspaper after we settled into our new digs. Doug was of another mind. He didn't see the need, and didn't want me to work outside of the home after we were married. This was a small point of contention, because I liked to work. I didn't want to argue, however, so I busied myself with sewing and writing journal type letters to both sides of the family.

I also took long walks, but sorely missed the companionship of a dog.

After we moved into our castle, I broached the subject of getting a dog. Doug was a cat person. He was not keen on the prospect of a dog in a trailer park. He brought up the point, and rightly so, that dogs lived on both sides and behind us. He won on the fact that we probably had enough dogs barking going on for the whole town of Kamiah just in our small neighborhood.

The request for a dog or puppy was denied. I was reluctantly in agreement.

That did not preclude cats, however.

I was not a cat person. I only owned a cat one time in my life. That did not end well. I found Charlie, a long haired older yellow male cat, in our garage one winter day.

Mom broke down and let me keep Charlie....well, at first. I truly loved old Charlie. Charlie did have his downsides. Evidently, Charlie had a terrible case of ear mites. Every time he shook his ears, his head would rattle. Charlie also liked to pee on everything outside. Mom didn't allow him in the house.

Mom did try to cure his ear mites. Many times she asked me to hold him while she poured mineral oil down his ears so he could shake his ears and spray the oil all over us. It didn't seem to help.

One day, Charlie was gone. Mom asked Dad to take him somewhere.

Two weeks later, Charlie was back, purring, meowing for food, rubbing my legs and shaking his rattling ears. I was so happy...for a couple of weeks.

Charlie was gone again. I was suspicious, but, no matter.

This time it only took a week for Charlie to come back. We were back to the old routine again. I guess Mom and Dad could see that Charlie really belonged with us!

Charlie disappeared again! I was in to the routine, this time and kept checking the garage for him to return. Return, he did. This time it took three weeks, but, by now, it was the middle of the summer and Charlie probably needed to make some stops on the way home.

Things settled in for the summer. I was home from school for summer vacation and had more time to spend with Charlie. Now, Charlie was really shedding and Mom decided that Charlie needed combing. Charlie would have none of it and bit my Mom.

Charlie disappeared again. I kept checking the garage all summer. Charlie never did return.

I finally told Doug that if it had to be a cat, we needed to go to Lewiston and get a cat.

Well, we didn't actually NEED to go to Lewiston to get a cat, but I really wanted a kitten, and it was January. After scouring all the local want ads and posters up in the local market, we decided our only option was to check out the Humane Society in Lewiston. We also needed to get our monthly groceries. For large items, it was a lot less expensive to purchase them at a big grocery outlet. The closest one of these would be sixty-two miles downriver at Lewiston.

When we got to Lewiston, it was covered in dense fog. This is not an unusual occurrence in mid-January in Lewiston, Idaho. Lewiston, Idaho is Idaho's only inland sea port. Large barges work their way up the Columbia River, through a system of locks into the Snake River to the port of Lewiston (At Lewiston, Idaho, the Clearwater River, which flows from the northeast, joins the Snake River, which flows from the Southwest. The barges haul grain and lumber downriver to ship overseas.

Lewiston, Idaho, founded in 1861 was the first capital of the Idaho Territory. It also boasts the lowest point in Idaho, which is located on the Snake River and is about 740 feet.

The other reason for the dense fog lay in Lewiston's largest industry, a large pulp mill, which processes logs into paper products. Over the last half a century, the paper exhaust from the paper mill has been vastly improved. Back in the 1969, the smell from the mill was a taint not easily forgotten. It hung over the city like an acrid blanket on most winter days. Only the winds of spring and uplifting air from the warm sun could melt the dense fog and lessen the acrid fumes.

Today, the smell from the plant is an afterthought and

not worth mentioning on most days. Lewiston is a beautiful town, full of color of its many beautiful fruit trees in the spring. The people are friendly and the town is brimming with history. I love to visit the Nez Perce Cultural Center just 11 miles upriver at Spalding. This combination museum and cultural center is filled with Nez Perce tribal artifacts and pictures. The Nez Perce, or Nimiipuu, have long been noted for their knowledge of horses. The Appaloosa Horse, (Idaho's Horse) breed was created from ponies the Nez Perce rode on the Palouse, (grasslands that are part of north central Idaho and southeastern Washington, which is also now famous for raising several varieties of grain. Much of the grain is barged out from Lewiston on the Clearwater to ocean ports at the headwaters of the Columbia River).

In a little valley to the south of the large pulp mill, we found the Lewiston Humane Society. It wasn't much back then. There were many cats and kittens in old wooden rabbit pens. They sat huddled, looking out through old chicken wire.

I saw my kitten. She was a little tiger striped ball of fur with large green eyes. I knew she was coming home with us the moment I set my eyes upon her.

On the ride home I had my first lesson in the difference between a puppy and a kitten. Puff began meowing

profusely. I decided she must have to "do her business".
I asked Doug to pull over so I could "take her potty".

I promptly got out at the side of the road and set her
down and told her to go potty...scratching her little paw
in the dirt. She scratched all four of her paws instead.
She drove like a four wheel drive jeep. With a meow
and a hiss she was out of there!

Luckily, she ran away from the highway. She crawled
under some train cars parked on a train track paralleling
the highway. I began to cry. Doug got out and calmly
walked over, crawled under the train car and retrieved
the confused kitten.

A few days after bringing her home, we had to visit the
local veterinarian. Puff had pneumonia. By the time she
was over the pneumonia, she was pretty bonded to us.

She would follow me like a dog on long walks. The local
dogs would run up, but Puff and I would stand our
ground and the dogs eventually gave up. When we
would go to town for groceries, we would let her
outside. When we came home, she was always waiting
for us at the top of the tree outside of our door.

We potty trained her to a box inside, but when she got
over her pneumonia, we put the potty box outside
under the trailer, because both of our parents taught us

that cats should do their "business", potty trained or not, out of doors.

The crazy thing is, though....I never did learn that cats just aren't supposed to go potty on the side of the road, either. Whenever we would head back up to the Silver Valley to visit with family, we would take Puff with us. She rode in the back seat, no cage, no leash. If she needed to go potty, she just mewed. We would stop and let her out for a walk. She would attend to business and we would head on down the road.

We also hauled that darned cat with us on other adventures around the area. Since visiting it the first time on Christmas Day, we made it a regular habit to take a drive up to see the progress on the building of Dworshak Dam. Dworshak lies on the north fork of the Clearwater River. It was the last large dam built in Idaho and was built for flood control and hydroelectricity generation. It was completed and opened in 1973. It is a concrete gravity dam and the third largest dam in the United States at 717 feet.

I remember how amazed we were at the size of the hole the water would fill and how small the equipment looked working on it. We made a promise to each other to visit this site again on our 50th anniversary.

Our cat, Puff lived with us for many years, shared many

adventures and welcomed our children into this world before her eventual demise. I still miss that cat.

As a side note, we did make a trip to the city of Pierce and Dworshak Dam this year (2020). The city of Pierce was the first county seat of Shoshone County, established in 1861 while Idaho was still part of the Washington Territory. The courthouse, built in 1862, still stands and is Idaho's oldest public building.

The Dent Bridge, crossing the North Fork of the Clearwater above the dam is a true work of art, reminiscent of the San Francisco Bridge. It appears as an apparition out of place and time with a paved road on one side and a dirt road leading to the beautiful little mountain town of Elk River on the other. It is a must see for the adventurous wanderer.

8

A Mountain Home with No Mountain

In early spring, Doug went off to school to train as an Idaho State Trooper. After he completed his four week course, he would be given a patrol car and a "residency", (location in the state where he would be stationed and be responsible for patrolling).

Puff, the cat and I waited in Kooskia in our 'castle'. We spent our days reading, sewing, and taking long walks. I also wrote letters daily, (no instant messages, no "Facetime", no "Facebook".) Phone calls were twice a week because there were long distance charges to consider.

I got to know some of our neighbors in the trailer court. They were all logging families. They had their opinions about Doug's job as part of law enforcement, especially since he was working at the weigh station that weighed their trucks, but they were nice, if a bit stand-offish.

One day a letter came from Doug, telling me that he was ready to graduate and where we would be moving for our 'station'.

 I was so excited, because the name of the town was Mountain Home! We were going to be able to stay in the mountains! He said it was east of Boise and there was a highway heading north out of Mountain Home that went to Hailey and Sun Valley.

Hey! That couldn't be too bad!

I ran next door to tell the neighbor lady where we would be moving. When I told her, her husband, a man with big boots, suspenders, an assortment of red plaid shirts and a big logging truck, was in the middle of removing those steel toed boots. He dropped one on his toe and let out a holler, followed by a roar of laughter.

His wife turned to offer him some sympathy about his toe, but he was having none of it. He was laughing too hard, and hopping about on one foot.

"Mountain Home, did you say Mountain Home? HA ha ha!"

"Well, little lady, you sure did get yourselves moved to the mountains, alright! You will be right comfortable when its 110 in the shade!"

"You can see the mountains, I guess...In the distance. Don't worry, though, there's plenty of sagebrush for wood, and a lot of rattlers and jack rabbits to eat when you get hungry."

9

From the Land of Mountains to the Land of Sage

I figure that logger must have done some logging on the headwaters of the Boise River above Mountain Home, because he sure was right about that town...well, kind of....but not quite.

The different thing about Mountain Home is that it stands, in the desert. It is about 10 miles away from the actual foothills of the Sawtooth Mountain range. The only trees are the ones planted and watered until they get their roots plenty deep. Most of those are deciduous. The closest river is the Snake, south of Mountain home by Bruneau, about 21 miles away.

 Rattlesnake creek rushes down from the mountains in the spring and fills Mountain Home reservoir for irrigation north of town. The creek dries to a trickle by the middle of July, but a lot of logging trucks still rumble out of the mountains above and through town.

Mountain Home started out as an Overland Stage Station called Rattlesnake Station. The location was about seven miles north of Mountain Home along Rattlesnake Creek just as you start into the foothills. It was a popular stage stop during the discovery of gold in the early 1860s.

About 1883, the location of the post office, (renamed Mountain Home, but close to the location of Rattlesnake Station), was moved down to the flats below to adjoin the railroad station. Mountain Home was founded.

Mountain Home airbase was opened in August of 1943. It has been a large influence on the economy of Mountain Home. Over the last forty years, Mountain Home has increasingly become a bedroom community to the ever growing Boise metropolis. I-84 goes through Mountain Home, bringing it ever closer to both Boise on the west and Twin Falls to the east.

It has the advantage of being able to still offer residents a home with country life within about 45 minutes of relatively big city amenities.

When we arrived in our little Ford Falcon, packed to the hilt, one evening in April, 1970, I was in shock. The town seemed the color of dusty gray green from the abundance of sage brush. It seemed flat as a pancake and as dry as an empty bathtub.

As we drove through town, I lit up as we passed the railroad park. Green lawn! Beautiful old green elm trees shaded the park with picnic tables and benches and sprinklers going. Not only was all the green a welcome sight, it was something I remembered from many years ago.

My family made a trip in our old school bus to see southern Idaho and our capitol building in Boise when I was about 13. We traveled through western Montana, through Stanley, down US 20 (SH68 at that time) and into Mountain Home, where our bus had some mechanical problems. I could remember the weather was really dry and hot.

Could we possibly be in that same town now? Was I ready to begin the next chapter in our life in the same town I remembered from so many years ago? I checked my memory by looking across the street from the railroad park. Yes! There was the filling station, and there was the water fountain we drank out of all those years ago!

The water seemed so fresh and cold on that hot day. I could remember telling my mother that I thought I would "live in this town someday!"

 My mother was quite upset, saying, "Why would you ever say something like that?"

I didn't know, except that the place seemed so restful after a hot day on the road with no air conditioning in the bus.

The desert town of Mountain Home, all of a sudden seemed full of hope and promise. Here was something familiar.

We passed under a train overpass and when the shadow of the overpass hit the car, I remembered a reoccurring dream I used to have after we took that trip in the school bus. I remembered the overpass because when we went under it with the old school bus I had been sleeping. A train crossed the overpass at that same moment, honking its horn. The sound of the train scared me awake. I jumped up to see the shadows it cast flashing overhead.

Somehow, again, this memory seemed to make me feel that things were more familiar and that I was meant to be here to complete some circle.

We made a long turn onto what they called "Airbase Road" which was (actually SH 67). Our trailer home, hauled all the way from Kamiah, Idaho was waiting for us only a few blocks away. The truck was there, with our home attached, ready to be set up in our lot. We would have to spend that night in a motel and see what the next day would bring.

10

Home is Where You Make It

It was amazing. Our home on wheels was already all set up. Of course, I needed to straighten furniture and unpack some boxes, but we were home again!

Now, I would like to take you on a little trip into the mountains north of Mountain Home so that you might understand why, besides the friends we made, this desert town left me with loving memories.

Mountain Home was originally founded along Rattlesnake Creek about ten miles north of the current site along old state highway 68, now US 20. It started as a stage stop and post office in the early 1880s, but was moved to its current site after the railroad was completed in 1883, so it would be closer to the railroad line. The name of Mountain Home moved out of the mountains with the town.

Mountain Home Airbase is a United States Air Force Base which was constructed in the early 1940s towards the end of World War II as a training base for bombers. After the war, the base was used for transports, then as a bomber and missile base. The missile sites were closed in 1964. In 1966 fighter planes replaced the bombers at Mountain Home Airbase.

In October 1991, Mountain Home became home to the 366th Fighter Wing with the mission to "develop and deploy combat-ready Airmen, take care of Gunfighters and protect and enhance our resources."

About 40 some odd miles north on old State Highway 68 (now US 20), the land gradually rises into the foothills of the Sawtooth Mountains, you will find Hill City, (which isn't much of a town, but maybe a gas station and some houses).   Not far before Hill City, a sign and a turn to the left takes you to Anderson Ranch Dam and reservoir on the South Fork of the Boise River.

Anderson Ranch Dam is a large earth filled dam built in 1941. It is a popular fishing, hunting and camping area. The Trinity Peaks in the Sawtooth Mountain Range stand above it beckoning adventurous hikers and tourists, and people, young and old, like us, looking for familiar mountains.

Some interesting little camping spots further up the South Fork of the Boise River are the towns of Pine, Featherville and Rocky Bar, still filled with the flavor of the old west and old gold mining lore. When we lived in Mountain Home, our favorite camping spot by far was Dog Creek Campground, north of Pine and south of Featherville.

If you are adventurous, you can take a road down the

South Fork of the Boise River from Anderson Ranch Dam, to the next dam on the river, Arrowrock Dam, which is a concrete arch dam and opened in 1915.

At 348 feet tall, Arrowrock was the highest Dam in the world when it was constructed. It took four years to build. It lies 42 miles downstream from Anderson Ranch Dam and about six miles upstream from the last hydroelectric dam on the south fork of the Boise River, Lucky Peak.

Lucky Peak Dam, reservoir and recreation area was created in 1955 for flood control, irrigation, recreation and hydroelectric use. It is still a popular spot in the summer for swimmers, boaters, fishermen, camping, and day hikers.

Another twenty some odd miles downstream lies Idaho's capitol city of Boise.

11

Life in the Meadows

Life as a state patrolman's wife in a small mobile home community in the early 1970s could be interesting.

I remember one evening I decided to make spaghetti, but was out of spaghetti, so I used elbow macaroni and created a sort of goulash.

Just as I finished the meal and set the table, I heard Doug pull up. I stepped out on the porch to greet him and noticed that he looked rather pale as he came up the path. I walked down to greet him and ask him what the matter was as he was pulling the evening paper from the box and shutting the gate. He mumbled something about just being at the scene of a suicide where a shotgun was involved. The only other thing I remembered was the word "head" as I turned and scurried into the house, mentioning that I thought I left the stove on.

I whisked the goulash off the stove and stuffed it in the oven just as he walked in the door. I mentioned to him that I hadn't started dinner yet, and asked what he felt like. I wasn't surprised to hear that he was passing on dinner.

I loved it when Doug worked night shift and would come home in the wee hours of the morning and tell me tales of some hunt in the desert for a driver that tried to ditch him, or of a "hit" (National Crime Information Center want record report) he received on the license plate of a car he stopped for stolen car, stolen gun or wanted felon. In the aftermath it sounded like a good crime mystery, not a potentially dangerous situation. We were young!

On his three day weekends we would take drives or go camping both north (into the Sawtooths and south of Mountain Home, along the Snake River. On these drives in the spring of 1970, it seems it was the "Year of the Rabbit" literally. Everywhere you drove in the desert, jack rabbits would run out in front of the car as you drove down the road. I would beg Doug to please "Miss them!"

He did some crazy dodging just to please me. Sometimes he would hit one, THUMP! Then, I would beg him to go back and "Please, finish it off!"

So he would. What a nut I was!

There was always something happening at the mobile park. Someone was moving in or moving out. Everyone was very friendly. In those days, probably about ninety percent of the people living at the Meadows Trailer Park were military. When my neighbors found out that my husband was a state patrolman, they said that we were "in the service" too, and included me as one of them in their activities. They took me out to the airbase to visit their "BX" or airbase exchange, and I would pay them to bring home pottery from their pottery shop on the base so I could paint pottery with them in the evenings when our husbands were working night shift.

The ladies were from all over the country and world. Many soldiers brought home brides from foreign tours of duty. Many of them were patiently waiting their husbands' return from the Vietnam War. It was a close group, and they made me feel at home. I still think fondly of many of them, a girl from Oregon who married a boy from Alabama, and was waiting for his return from Vietnam so they could settle on his parent's farm in Alabama. Another was a lady from Germany and her two little girls. Her husband was also in Vietnam. His home was Florida. A large family of seven lived next to us. They were a busy happy group of a mother and five children waiting for husband and father to also return from Vietnam. Many returned and left with their families to new assignments before we moved our mobile home to its own piece of land the next spring.

The warmth of those families in Meadows Mobile Court coupled with the fact that I started editing and writing the court newspaper, "the Meadows Echo" during our stay there kept me from missing home too much.

The Meadows Echo was a simple little bulletin of about five or six pages, mimeographed on light green typing paper. It usually included recipes, poems, stories, handy hints or court bulletins and for sale items and a kids' page. It came out once a month. I loved creating that little bulletin. It gave me a chance to write, to interact with people, to learn new things, and to keep busy.

I also found that I could work part-time as assistant for a local orthodontist when his regular girl was ill or needed a day off.

That winter I discovered a large pond in the desert out behind the mobile park.

If I had been more familiar with desert topography, I might have questioned the origins of such a pond, but I was used to seeing ponds and rivers, so I really didn't give it much thought. There were trees and bushes around it, and it reminded me of home. I loved watching geese land on it or fly up and off, calling to each other.

I unpacked my ice skates and often went down there to skate on the ice when it got thick in the middle of the winter.

The next spring as things began to thaw I found the origins of the pond. It was the overflow settling pond for the mobile park septic system.

12

Our Very Own

That next spring Doug's partner and senior resident patrolman in Mountain Home, Del Foster, and his wife Rosalie convinced us to move our mobile home out to our very own piece of land.   We were really anxious to own our own home, and putting our mobile home on a solid foundation, making it a permanent fixture seemed like a good solution.

We found an acre and a third of land in a subdivision northwest of town for $750. The subdivision was called appropriately "Someday Subdivision". We began the process of readying our piece for the arrival of our mobile home. The costs were adding up and we were worried about the budget. Del and Rosie lived on a large ranch north of Mountain Home and had a farm tractor. They brought it down to help. They set a mobile home up on their ranch, so were practiced in creating septic tanks and drain fields. We drew out a plan for the inspector, and he Okayed it. We set to work, the four of us. The tractor helped immensely with the digging of the lines and the hole for the septic tank. We formed up a septic tank and hired a concrete truck come in and pour the floor, walls and a top. We ran the lines and finished our septic system.

A local well drilling company, Hiddleston Well Drilling, brought in the first drill rig I had ever seen. This was one of the old ones, a cable rig, with a motor that lifted a large pointed bit up then down pounding the earth like a pick. Then the operator would attach a long cylinder, pour water in the hole and send the cylinder down to suck up the loosened muddy earth and dump it out. It was a slow process, bang bANg BANGing away, but it worked.

Amazingly, one day we came out to find water flowing. We had our own well! It was 135 feet deep. This was quite novel to us at the time. We were used to springs and gravity flow water.

Power was brought in and a pump was put in the well.

The freeway was under construction through Mountain Home at the time. That section of the freeway was poured concrete slabs. When they were finished with the pouring of the concrete, the batch plant out by the freeway was torn down and moved. We used to ride our bikes out on the section of unopened freeway that spring. We discovered there was a great deal of un-bagged concrete just left lying on the ground as waste where the plant had been set up.

We would go out there and collect the concrete, hand mix it with gravel and water in a cement mixer and created footings for the mobile home and a slab to put our water storage tank and pump plumbing on. We found a shed for sale in the local want ads and hauled it in on a snowmobile trailer, placing it on the slab over the plumbing.

We were ready for our mobile home to be moved in on its foundation.

One morning, early in May of 1971, our mobile home sat on our own piece of land. We were now a solid piece of Mountain Home, Idaho.

13

Nothing is Perfect

You can't really loose something that doesn't belong to you in the first place. You can't really loose something that will be with you beyond all time and place. You can only loose the feeling that you are in control and able to keep bad things from happening. I think that is called loss of innocence and loss of total trust.

I was fortunate. Life stayed relatively innocent and trustworthy for the greater part, for me, until I was twenty-three years old. In retrospect, I think of young men who went to war for this country in their teens and woke up to this feeling out on the battlefield, watching their comrades die, or waking up in a field hospital amidst the suffering. I think of children born into suffering in third world nations. Some children possibly have never have known a safe situation where they could even know the meaning of the words safe or trust. Those two words are largely assumed in the most American homes. I didn't realize that you should always question, not assume.

When I first found I was pregnant, I was overjoyed. I patiently waited for this time, making sure that my husband and I had a strong foundation to build our family on. I married at 21, with a small savings and a profession to fall back upon, should the financial need arise. My husband was happy in his job as a State Policeman, and we were now settled on our own piece of land, with our mobile home no longer mobile. We were ready to take the next step in life.

I made my first doctor appointment and launched into preparing for the blessed event. This was early spring, 1971. It was so exciting. I was started on prenatal vitamins, and the next appointment was set for a check-up.

A great source of support was the other State Patrolman's wife, Rosalie. They also lived in Mountain Home. She was a lifelong resident of the area and the granddaughter of rancher, Cordie Hoffman, who was born in Atlanta, Idaho in 1895 to a couple who owned a grocery store in Rocky Bar and operated a freight line from Rocky Bar to Boise. Rosie was a wealth of information and helped me out like a big sister. Rosie and Del could relate stories Cordie told them of riding with his father on the big horse-drawn wagons to Boise and back. The trip took upwards of a month at times to complete. He also related selling bottles of soda to the miners for a nickel a bottle.

Del, her husband, was like a big brother to both my husband and I. He met Rosie while stationed at

Mountain Home Airbase.

Rosie and Del were as excited as Doug and I were about the coming event. They had a sweet little daughter about four years old. I think everyone that met their little girl spoiled her a little. She was so loveable and smart! She was also looking forward to the new baby, and would ask each time we visited, how much longer it would be before she had a playmate.

As spring neared, I busied myself with planting trees and bushes, and making a garden. I packed a great deal of my water to outlying bushes and trees, trying to be careful to limit the weight, yet knowing that exercise was also good for me.

We had a young dog that would follow me around. I continually needed to watch him, though, because he had a habit of wandering off, and a penchant for trying to catch the neighbor's roosters that would wander to the edges of our property.

A spring moved towards summer. In Mountain Home, being desert, the days had already started to get dry and hot by the middle of June. I packed more water, kept the garden weeded, read more books and stayed in during the hotter parts of the day. My feet began to swell as well as my stomach. I found myself tiring much easier, and falling to sleep early in the evenings.

Pregnancy was new to my husband. He was an only child. It was just as new to our best friends and confidents, Rosie and Del. My checkups with the doctor continued every 6 weeks. He cautioned me to not work in the heat of the day and to be sure I was taking my vitamins and not to eat salty things. He paused a bit and said that he was thinking about putting me on pills to reduce my water retention, but thought better of it, and said he figured if I just cut out salt, it would do the trick.

In the next couple of weeks, I began wearing an old pair of Doug's shoes since I could no longer get mine on my feet. I called my mother and asked her about swelling. She carried seven children, but never experienced much swelling with any of them. She said to just watch my salt intake, put my feet up when resting and ask the doctor at the next appointment.

Looking back, I see I did not ask enough questions or talk to my doctor enough. I also could have gone to the library and read up on water gain with pregnancy. I could have done so much. I actually just thought it was probably pretty normal and I didn't want to be a complainer

On the evening of July 3, Doug was working the late shift. I didn't have much appetite and went to bed early. I woke to a shock. Something burst inside and the bed was drenching wet. I was experiencing terrible pains and knew the baby was coming early. I called dispatch to have Doug come home and called the hospital. They told me to come in as soon as possible, that I was going to have a "dry birth" at best. They said I probably lost all of the amniotic fluid around the child. I was scared to death.

Everything is pretty much a blur after that. I just remember being on the table in the delivery room. The doctor said she was coming and nothing was stopping it. He made a larger vaginal incision which hurt more than her coming out. In a moment she was there, dark hair, large brown eyes looking at me.

I expected him to hand her to me. Instead, he wrapped her in a blanket and put her into an incubator and she was wheeled out of the room before I could even touch her.

I cried, "Let me see my baby! Let me just see her! Let me just touch her!"

The nurse pushed me back down on the table. I fought back. My baby needed me! Why couldn't they just let me touch her!

The nurse called in two orderlies, who held me down without saying anything. She shoved a needle into my arm. The world faded away.

A little over two and a half hours later I awoke to Doug and Del discussing things in the corridor outside my room. Del was saying he thought they could get a plane from Boise to fly Julee to Salt Lake City. (At the time, there was no NICU care center in Boise). I knew Julee was born early and that she was small. I figured it must have something to do with her breathing, although I knew she was breathing when they took her away.

General Hospital was playing on a television in my room. It was weird. It was a hospital scene and, I think Laura, (Luke's other half)…or somebody on the show, just had a baby on the show and lost it. I thought, in a bleary drunken way…"ha ha…MY baby will live!"

The nurse told Del and Doug that I was awake. They both came in. Del was in his uniform. Doug reached for my hand. I noticed his hand was much warmer than mine. Before they could say anything, the doctor and two nurses came in. The doctor and one nurse looked like they had been crying.

"I am sorry to tell you that your daughter has just passed away of a massive heart attack".

I don't remember much more, just that another nurse came in and gave me a shot to dry up my milk.

They sent me home the next day, the 4th of July, 1971.

We told the doctor we wanted to have an autopsy. Everyone said "This happens a lot with first babies, you will get over it. Just don't think about it."

I told the nurses I understood, I told them what I thought they wanted to hear, what would make them just go away. I told them that I would be fine.

I didn't feel fine. I talked to my mother. She had no experience with loosing babies. She had produced seven beautiful babies. I couldn't even produce one.

She said, "Just put it out of your mind and be glad you didn't see her more than just a glimpse, you would just remember her as something dead. You need to forget."

I wanted a funeral, but neither set of parents could come down. My parents still had several children at home and my father worked his regular job plus other side jobs. I understood.

I went in a daze to fireworks at Mountain Home that night. I sat on a blanket on a sparse lawn in the park. I remember looking at the dry grass. The color of it, waving in the breeze looked and felt just as dry as my baby somewhere in a morgue.

I wasn't there for her when she needed me most. I failed to protect her. What kind of a mother was I?

I didn't cry. It was a long time before I was able to shed those tears. Now, I still do at times.

We made funeral arrangements the following day, pending release of the body. I thought we would have a church service. We were members of the Catholic Church in Mountain Home. I was secretary/treasurer for the priest who had just retired. A new priest now filled his spot.

When we checked with him, he advised us that there would be no Catholic service. According to him, we never thought to call him to do last rites, so no Church service. We protested, saying that the head nurse was Catholic and advised us that she performed last rites.

He said this was not good enough, and she would not have services in the Church.

We held graveside services. I followed my mother's suggestion and never looked at my child at the mortuary, fearing it would affect my life forever if I saw her in that state.

I left instructions to have her wrapped in the beautiful blanket my mother-in-law knitted for her. We bought her a beautiful headstone and tucked her into the ground.

It took us a lot more of this book and many years to

finally be at peace with this moment in time. Remember, there was an autopsy. Life is learning. Time is healing.

14

Finally, My Baby

Fourteen months after we lost Julee, our son was born. He came out hollering! The nurses insisted he lay on his stomach. He didn't want to lie on his stomach, he wanted to crawl. The hospital had a rule in those days that babies needed to lie on their stomach to keep them from choking and you could not see your baby for 12 hours after you gave birth. It sounded crazy to me, and still does. I wanted my baby! My baby wanted me.

I heard a commotion in the hallway when I woke up, frustrated, about 6 hours into the ordeal. I asked a passing nurse what the problem was. She admitted that our baby loosened his tie on his navel by trying to crawl and flaying around screaming in his bassinette and it was bleeding. She assured me that it was taken care of and he was now lying on his side propped up.

I slept. Six hours later my baby was brought to me. I was never so happy in my life. We went home a few hours later.

It was a good thing I slept in the hospital. He was colicky. I was still learning to nurse. Breast nursing was still pretty much not the thing. Most people were still bottle feeding, the turnabout to breast nursing was just starting. I asked a nurse in the hospital to help me. She looked at me like I was crazy and said, "I don't know anything about that sort of stuff. You'll just have to do the best you can if that is what you want to do".

So I did.

Six weeks later, my doctor, told me that I was giving my son colic because he was drinking nervous milk. He convinced me to stop breast feeding and start bottle feeding my baby. I still had a colicky baby until he was between 3 and 4 months old.

I gradually learned that my own intuition was better than asking the doctor for simple things. We settled into a comfortable and happy routine.

Our son was a busy, happy and determined baby. Before he walked, he was happiest riding around in a backpack on my back. He slept better there too. He was born in September. By the time the grasses came out in the spring, he was on his way to walking. He started walking at seven and one half months. He never crawled.

In the early summer we would take camping trips south of Mountain Home to Bruneau, a farming community along the Snake River. In the summer green fields line the Snake, irrigated by huge overhead automatic wheel sprinkler lines. The sight is spectacular. Protected by high plateaus surrounding the river valley, cattle graze contentedly late into the year.

Between Bruneau and Murphy(the county seat of Owyhee County with a population of under 100 citizens according to the 2020 census), is the Cove Campground.

The Cove campground is a quiet tree-lined back-water cove along the Snake River.   The water is warm and inviting and not very deep. The campground was built after the Second World War by Civilian Conservation Core workers. It was the perfect place to teach a 7 month old baby to swim. He took to the water like a little fish. We later taught our daughter the same way.

Another place we used to visit heading east between Bruneau and Hammett, Idaho was the Bruneau Dunes State Park.

Here lie sand dunes that will make you believe you are in the Mohave Desert! We used to take flat cardboard and slide down the dunes. (I believe now you can rent special boards for this). There are even equestrian facilities at the dunes if you have horses.

The nicest thing I think they have added in the years since the children were young is an observatory. You can check the internet for hours.

They used to say that in Mountain Home, the only time the wind stops is to change directions. In the winter, the wind would blow against the back of our mobile home and make the end wall, which was in our bedroom, squeak. If you listened to it long enough, it sounded like a song the wind sang. I tried to turn the creak, creak into some soft words, but it never came out as soft words, just more creaking.

Doug got thinking about that creak. Frustrated, one day he went out with his hammer and a wedge. He drove a wooden wedge in between the roof and the wall. Amazing! The creak was fixed! It was hard to go to sleep that night. No creak.

15

Rattlesnake Creek

One day in early March 1973, Doug came home to announce that we would be building a new home. He was out picking up some supplies at Jim's Lumber and became engaged in a conversation about a new subdivision that was being built by Jim Alexander, the owner of the lumber company.

Doug was convinced that this was the time and place to build the house he always wanted to build. The subdivision consisted of acre parcels of land and was located only about three miles east from where we lived as the crow flies.

I was not happy! We were comfortable in our current home. We had a really fair payment. We owned our car. We were just starting to get a savings built up. Why now?

Doug was adamant. He explained that it was a really good chance to have a stick built house. He said he always dreamed of building a house and since a lot of people were moving into Mountain Home, and the airbase was growing, it was a good time to sell our present home.

I wasn't convinced, but I went along with it. We put an ad in the paper and before we knew it, our home was sold and our new home was barely started. Where were we to live?

Our friends, Delmar and Rosalie had a solution. They owned a small rental house on their ranch. It was perfect. We now lived in a very small two bedroom little house on the edge of Rattlesnake Creek along SH 68 (now US20). The place had a nice little yard with a lawn and bushes. I used to take our baby son out on the lawn on hot summer days so he could play with the hose. We were out in the farm fields. I would strip off his cloths, turn on the hose very low and he would play in the water and drink out of the hose. He was only about 8 months old and waddled when he walked across the lawn, falling on his behind and giggling every so often. Our little dog, Josie, a Pomeranian, would play with him, getting just as wet.

One hot afternoon, I just finished putting a clean diaper on the baby and put him down for a nap. Our little dog, Josie was barking off and on since I came in the house. I looked out the window and she was barking at the bush our baby had been playing by. I went out to see what the problem was and heard a very large rattling noise. There, curled up under the bush where my baby had just been playing was a big rattlesnake.

Doug was working, but our neighbor, Delmar, the other state policeman was at home in their mobile home just across from our house. I rushed over and got him. He brought out his 357 and blasted that rattlesnake good.

That was the first rattler I had ever seen. I hoped it would be the last. It wasn't.

Two weeks later, I was visiting Rosalie in her home. The Fosters had a son a matter of months older than ours. Both boys were playing on the floor. Their daughter was playing with them. Del had been up at the barns. He came in with a very large angle worm in a jar.

"Come here, I want you to see something." He said.

I went over and looked in the jar. The kids gathered around.

I said, "That's an awfully big worm!"

Rosalie laughed and explained that it was no worm at all. It was a baby rattler, just hatched. They explained that is when rattlers are most dangerous. Not only do they not have any rattlers, but they can't control the amount of venom they inject.

I have since learned that is a myth, but any rattlesnake is extremely dangerous large or small. The idea that baby rattlers are more dangerous came from the old belief that generally follows the idea that the young rattlers can't control the amount of venom they inject meaning they will inject everything they have. According to the Natural History Museum of Los Angeles County in California, bigger snakes have bigger venom sacks, so even if a young rattler can't control its venom, which there is some question about, a larger rattlesnake would have more venom to inject if it so wished.

16

The Piggy Built a House of Brick

Our house was raising itself up out of the ground. It was to be a house of brick with no walls to squeak in the wind.   The contractor we hired allowed us to work under him to perform certain jobs on the house. One of those jobs was painting on the inside. Another was shingling the roof. By the time we were on the roof shingling it, I already knew I was pregnant with our third child.

We moved into our new brick house August 1, 1973. We spotted in bricks from a railroad roundhouse that my dad had torn down in our hometown of Wallace. We felt that we still had a part of our hometown with us that way. The chimney for the fireplace was totally made from those bricks and was created with a unique design. Our builder really liked to make individualistic chimneys. The house wasn't large, but was really warm and homey. It was 1200 square feet, with a 2 car garage. It stands proudly today. The chimney is still a masterpiece.

The carpenter was just finishing up some touch up work as I unpacked and hand washed my dishes in the kitchen before putting them into the new cupboards. He kept watching me. Finally he stated that he just couldn't watch any longer. He wanted to know just what I was doing hand washing everything when I had a dishwasher.

I never owned a dishwasher before and I was hesitant to start using it at first. I explained that I didn't mind hand washing dishes and the dishwasher would probably be used for big meals, but I didn't see why get in a hurry to use it.

Exasperated, he asked if he could help by showing me how to run it and place dishes. Ha! Pretty good planning! I just got some kitchen help! He was great. He showed me how to operate the dishwasher, which really wasn't that hard, and the whys and how of placing the dishes and silverware.

My dishwasher and I have been best friends ever since.

17

Another Baby

Seventeen months after our son was born, I gave birth to our second daughter. Doug's father broke his hip while working in Moscow, Idaho as a bank auditor the same evening that I went in to labor.

Our daughter was born with an omphalocele. The omphalocele was not large, only about the size of a quarter.

I had a new doctor. I changed doctors when I found out I was pregnant this time. Our second daughter was born full term, all eight pounds twelve ounces of her! The doctor was prepared. I told him of the loss of my first baby. He had no desktop computer, but he possessed a great library of books. He researched all the information he could find.

Our doctor called NICU at St. Lukes and a pediatrician and ambulance from St. Lukes arrived soon after. An omphalocele can be a pretty serious matter, but our little daughter received excellent care at St. Lukes Hospital NICU.

However, what sounded like just a matter of checking her for further defects and sewing her up, turned into many days of worrying and a wait and see project after having to disturb her entire digestive system in exploratory surgery. This was the only option to insure there were no more problems since they did not have available to them any of the medical imagery we have available today.

She was alert and wanted to eat, but could not keep anything down. The doctors explained that as a result of the operation, her system experienced a major shock. It would take time for her digestive system to get back on track.

I went home from the hospital the day after our daughter was born and sent to St. Lukes NICU in Boise. We packed up our young son and went in to Boise to stay with Doug's parents. We left our little boy at home with his grandparents and went directly to the hospital to see our infant daughter in NICU.

We were surprised that the nurses encouraged us to touch her, talk to her as much as possible. We could actually see her little heart monitor react when we talked to her.

Since his father was in the hospital in Moscow, Doug drove his mother to Moscow the next day. I stayed at their house with our little boy. The next afternoon, I took our son with me to the hospital. The nurses held him while I talked to the baby and touched her. Our little boy watched from the glass window with the nurse.

That night Doug flew back in from Moscow. His mother was staying with his father in Moscow after his operation to pin his hip.

Our baby continued to not be able to keep fluids down for 21 days. They fed her intravenously a special fluid that was developed at the University of Portland. Frustrated, we watched as our baby stayed alive and alert, but lost a few ounces each day. Each time they tried to feed her water from a bottle it came back up.

There were a few more "hitches".

While our infant was being fed intravenously, they moved the needle inserted in her vein around to new spots often to keep the veins from collapsing. While she was being fed from a vein in the foot, the vein collapsed, sending the fluid under the skin, causing a burn on the top of her foot an inch and a half by an inch.

It was pretty traumatic to come back in to see our baby lying there with her leg all bandaged up.

She was a trooper, though, and handled it well. A skin graft operation would be needed in the near future.

The other hitch was that she developed a staph infection

in her sutures. Although the outer stitches held, she developed a large hernia on her abdominal area.

I worried about this when she cried, but it didn't seem to bother her and they wanted her to grow and gain weight before they closed the hernia.

On the 21st day the decision was made to allow me to start breast feeding her. It worked! She acted like she had been nursing all along. Once she began eating, it was only days before she went home.

As soon as she gained the appropriate amount of weight, she had plastic surgery to fix the burned area on the top of her foot.

With all of these things, you would think that our child's development would be delayed. Although she stayed small in stature, it did not slow her down. She began crawling at about seven and a half months, and began walking by nine months.

At nine months she went back in to close her herniated area.

I learned that we were far from being the only parents that have not experienced textbook beginnings with childbirth. After spending time in the hospital children's ward, I felt fortunate. I saw so many children and babies in the ward that had to have open heart surgery, repair of cleft lip and/or palate, conjoined twins. These are only a few things that send infants to the NICU and to surgery. I also saw that the infants and toddlers dealt with their situation better than the parents. Whatever the concern was, it was their normal.

Toddlers in for second and third operations can't wait to be well enough to be wheeled in little red wagons to the children's play room to get on with being a child.

Just to keep everyone from worrying, or looking ahead in the book, our children never slowed down. Early years of trauma were replaced by happy, studious children, interested in programming the new Commodore Computers of the late 1980s and early 1990s, 4-H programs and Dungeon and Dragons, horseback riding, Little League and dance classes.

18

We Planted Trees and Houses

I always liked the story of Johnny Appleseed. I think we just decided to take his story to another level. Why not plant houses WITH the trees?

Again, I set to planting trees, pine, fruit, shade, bushes, and roses, many old yellow hedge roses. Our yard flourished. I still can go back and see trees, actually too many trees surrounding the house.

I loved my yard. I also raised a vegetable garden, chickens and rabbits.

However, when our daughter was born and we were staying in Boise, dogs broke through our pasture fencing (four foot tall, square wired horse fencing), and through the second fenced area where our chickens and rabbits were and slaughtered them. A few chickens escaped and went to a neighboring farm. We left them there when we got home.

Early, the following spring, Doug accepted a transfer to Meridian, Idaho. It was a beautiful area with more trees, more water, just greener. It also would be closer to his parents in Boise.

We sold the beautiful little brick house in March of 1975.

We found a home on the outskirts of Meridian on an acre and were excited about closing on the home and moving. We received a call from Doug's supervisor.

Budget cuts in the government caused all transfers to be cancelled. Doug's transfer was off.

Our home was sold. Our furniture was moved to his parent's basement in anticipation of closing on our new home. We quickly found a rental in our old mobile home court, the Meadows.

We moved in April of 1975. We were back where we started, but renting. The upside was that we had money in the bank. When we sold our home, we doubled the money we invested in a little over a year. Transfers were out, so the question was, did we bide our time in a rental or try our luck at something else?

One morning in early May I awoke with an idea. I turned to Doug, who was just waking up.

"You know that land out by the reservoir north of Mountain Home that we drove out by a while back? Remember the sign that said 5 acre parcels for 5,000?"

"What would you say if I said I think we should buy one of those parcels and build a home on it? You know, we have learned a lot about building. I'll bet we could do a lot of it ourselves. You can plumb and wire, and we learned how to shingle a roof. In fact, I'll tell you what, if you agree to this, I'll shingle the roof if you do the wiring and plumbing."

Doug says to this day that last statement was what got him thinking.

"Well, why not."

Pretty soon we were plotting and planning. We drove out and looked at the land again in a serious manner. We checked want ads and found a second (well, third or fourth) hand beat up 8 foot trailer to haul out to the land to live in.

We purchased the land, (actually two five acre parcels), called Hiddleston Well Drilling, who by that time were friends with us, and started drilling a well on our land. This time we got to watch a new rotary rig drill away. It went much faster for a time. We felt just like pioneers. This was actually a raw piece of desert land that had never been lived on by anyone other than possibly a passing sheep herder or an Indian family from another era.

And then it happened. No water. The hole we drilled was a dry hole.

As it happened, we chose to drill the well at the top end of our property. That area was on top of an underground ridge of basalt that rode above the underground lake of water much like an overhanging cliff might over a channel of water below. Water was there, but the area we chose was not the quickest route by far.

The Hiddlestons were sympathetic. They reduced the price of drilling the hole by half and backfilled it.

They moved the drill down the property towards the road about 200 feet and started again.

This time we had success! They hit the cleanest purest water at 250 feet. The flow was great! We had plenty of water for the house and for irrigation. We were ready to build.

This time we hired the septic built. We got our house plans approved and the foundation in so we could have the pump and wiring placed in the garage area. Now all the basics were installed. We could hook up the old trailer, clean it up and live in it while the house was being built.

By the time we got all of this done, it was the first part of July. We said goodbye once again to Meadows Mobile Park and moved out onto our acreage below the Mountain Home reservoir north of town.

A lot of work needed to be done before winter.

The trailer was anything but beautiful. It was a faded yellow and white with aluminum silver color showing through with years of wear. There was the master bedroom to the very back, with a hallway on the left side by the doors that ran all the way to the front dining area. In between was a small bedroom, about the size of a medium walk-in closet and a bathroom. The dining room was next with a kitchen in front. It was basically all we needed, but would become mighty close as the heat of the summer pushed through to the winds and rain in the fall and the biting cold of winter setting in.

We hired the framing done, and the roofing sheets put on. While Doug got to work on the plumbing and wiring, I got the trailer arranged and got the kids, dog and cat (Puff) settled in.

The dog was a young pup, Jessie, whom I picked up at a shelter in Hayden Lake when I was visiting my sister. She held a job as a newspaper reporter and was writing an article on an animal shelter. I tagged along and was walking around the shelter looking at dogs when a female pup caught my eye.

She was sitting, looking off with what for all the world, seemed like a look of total disdain. Other dogs were barking and howling. It looked like she thought that she was too good for the likes of them, so she determined to staunchly remain immune to this mistreatment and in control of the situation. I couldn't help but love her in that moment.

Jessie was supposed to be half German shepherd and one half Shetland sheepdog. She probably was because she certainly looked like both breeds, and a little like a coyote. I decided we probably needed a dog to keep the coyotes away and warn us of snakes on that wild piece of land. She would do.

Jessie did come in handy. She followed us around as we wandered our land and the BLM acreage out back. She herded the kids if they wandered too far. She warned us of snakes. She barked when coyotes came near. She listened to my joys and my complaints. She became my best friend.

It was time to shingle the roof. The sheets of plywood were on the roof and the house was being sided. Doug and a couple of hired men were working on the siding together. When the kids went down for their naps in the morning, I would start shingling. When our little boy came to the door and hollered, I knew he was up and the baby would be fussing to get out of her bed/playpen.

I also set up a playpen outside the house in the shade. The baby would go in the playpen and our little man would follow Doug around and "help" until he got underfoot. Then we would give him a tiny hammer and nails. An old wooden step ladder served well as his "project". He would spend up to 20 minutes hammering nails into that step ladder, for Doug to pull them out later. Up until about two years ago, we kept that step ladder with many of the nails still hammered into it!

The children also had a sand pile out in back of the house with trucks and toys. When they got fussy, and the day was nice, I would bring the playpen out back in the shade by the sandbox and they would talk to each other, and share toys.

Many times I would come down to check on them to find the baby also had part of the sandbox in her playpen, contentedly playing with some sandy toys he shared with her, while her rattle or stuffed toy was being carted off in a toy truck.

Doug finished the plumbing and wiring and came up to help me with the last piece of roofing. The roofing job was fairly easy because the roof was straight runs, but tedious and slow because I went up and down so many times checking on children. By mid October, the house was nearing completion and none too soon!   There were less days the children could be out of doors. We were working on flooring, painting and finish work. The kids now could be kept in one of their large bedrooms, where we would pile a bunch of their toys and turn them loose.

Doug wanted to build all of the kitchen cabinets, but in the end, we ordered custom made so that we could get the house finished and close out the construction loan that was a high interest rate. Our house and land cost us a total of $62,000.

We moved in the middle of November 1975, just before Thanksgiving. It was cold out. We knew that winter was on its way. I can remember going out to help Doug drill some last minute holes for wiring in the garage. That was the first time I used a drill with a three-quarter inch bit for drilling wiring holes. I was pushing the drill into the wood timber as the wind howled outside, saying to myself, "I am in Siberia! I am a Russian laborer in a camp of tents in Siberia drilling through the ice!"

I guess it was cold! The hole broke through. I went in to check on the kids sleeping contentedly in their new warm bedrooms.

The trailer was already sold to a farm in Grandview, Idaho for immigrant labor housing. They came out the day after we moved into the house to haul it away.

We were home once again.

19

Settling In

Our home truly seemed like a gigantic castle, coming from eight months in a two small trailer homes. This house was 1600 square feet with an oversized two car garage. Ten acres of rocky desert land went with it plus BLM land that ran for miles out our back door. We truly were in paradise.

A warm Franklin stove served as added warmth to the living room. In the kitchen a little pot bellied stove, just for atmosphere, served as a great way to add a little moisture to the dry air during the winter. I kept a small kettle of water simmering away on the stove during cold windy days. I could also get up in the morning and cook pancakes, eggs and little pig sausages on the wood stove just like my parents did when we were kids. There is nothing like breakfast over a wood cook stove!

Spring comes early in the desert. One day the wind was howling and the snow was coming down. The next day, the wind changed direction. It had a soft, springy feel. The desert flowers erupted and the birds begin to sing.

We planted lawn, trees and bushes in front of the house with a vegetable garden on the south side of the house. Out the back door on the lawn were a couple of big shade trees, with a proper sandbox and a wooden six foot fence fully enclosing the backyard.

My paternal grandparents lived on a ranch on the North Fork of the Coeur d'Alene River. They used to have a very large rope swing made from logs about 15 feet tall with a crossbar. I missed that swing. We decided that our kids should have a swing like that. Doug built a facsimile off to the side of the driveway. That swing was a hit with both adults and kids.

We started going for long walks over our land and into the desert. Our dog, Jessie, and Puff the cat followed everywhere. Our son wore little cowboy boots and a little cowboy straw hat, many times a six pistol in his little holster. Our daughter usually rode on the backpack on my back. She was getting around fine on her own, but when walking through sagebrush, it was just easier. She was small and had a time picking through the sage.

On one walk that spring, we were traveling along our fence line to the south. There were old wooden moving storage boxes to the back of the neighboring property. I knew there were some old cats that lived in them, and we heard meowing like kittens. The man that owned the property worked on the airbase and came out the property infrequently.

I had heard a rattlesnake before, but that one was very clear, and I had no doubt what or who he was before I set my eyes on him. This time, and probably because it was farther off, it sounded like maybe some dry rattling, almost like leaves. The sound made me wary, especially because of the last run in with a rattler. I still wasn't sure that I didn't imagine what I was hearing, but it sounded like it could be coming from the boxes by the fence. Our son was headed that direction, so I took his hand and lead him back over away from the fence. We veered off and headed back to the house. It was lunch time anyway, and I had an uneasy feeling about what I heard.

The next afternoon the kids and I were out in back of our house when the neighbor man pulled up in his pickup. He got out and told me to come over to the pickup so he could show me something. I looked over the back of the pickup to see the biggest fattest snake I had ever seen! No kidding, that thing was probably swollen five inches around. When stretched out, it was about four feet long.

He said, "I see you out wandering with those two little kids out there. I just wanted you to know what is out in this desert. This one has a friend out there too. It just ate my cat's kittens that were in that old box out there. He is still digesting and was slow. That's why I got him."

That really had an impact on me. We still went out in

the desert, but now I knew for sure what to listen for and watch for.

We did have a few more snake encounters, but thankfully, they were with bull snakes. Probably the reason for this was we found we were lucky. We inherited some protectors. A pair of bull snakes decided to make a den under our house. It is said that bull snakes will chase rattlesnakes away. I don't know if that is so, but it worked for us.

One day in the spring, our little boy was on his tricycle playing on our back patio. All of a sudden I heard a high pitched scream. I looked out the patio doors to see a very large snake strung out sunning himself under his tricycle. He sat on the seat on his tricycle staring at the snake and bawling.

I panicked, yet felt a cold calm cover me. I slowly slid the sliding glass door open talking to our son all of the time. I kept my eye on the lazy snake as I talked to calm him down and reach for a shovel by the door.

"Now, I know he looks scary, but I want you to be as still and quiet as you can. He is not going to hurt you. He is just enjoying the sunshine. Now, you see how his head is all straight with no big fat jaws? And see, there are no rattles on his tail. That means he is probably just an old bully snake. He won't hurt you. He is just out looking for mice."

He stopped crying and was listening. I reached over and swooped him off his tricycle and into the doorway. I scooped with the shovel, picking up the snake while he draped over the blade, just realizing his nap had been interrupted.

I swung him as hard as I could over the back fence. It must have been a mighty shock for that snake being wakened so rudely from his sunny nap as he hit the hard ground!

We saw the pair of bull snakes occasionally after that, but never saw any more rattlers. The bull snakes never napped under his tricycle again and we never aimed our hike out toward the storage boxes near the corner of our property.

20

The Teton Dam Bursts

Doug received a call on the afternoon of June 5 1976. The Teton Dam in southeastern Idaho broke at 11:57 in the morning. The dam lay above the town of Sugar City, and in bursting, sent ninety-four billion gallons of water rushing downstream. The result was massive flooding downstream taking out homes, businesses, farmland, secondary and primary highways and bridges.

The damage to structures and farmland was shocking. Thirteen thousand cattle and many other farm animals were lost. The loss of human lives was surprising, not in a negative way but in a positive way. Eleven people were killed. The fact of the low number deaths was attributed to the time of day.

One harrowing tale was related in the local newspaper about a man that was fishing in the Teton River about two miles below the dam. He noticed the river was rising at an incredible rate. In a matter of minutes the water rose approximately six feet. He looked upstream and saw a wall of water about thirty feet high heading in his direction. He ran away from his fishing spot, but was caught by the outer waves and washed into the current. He was able to ride it out on a log. Somewhere along the ride, his log crashed into another log breaking some of his ribs and puncturing a lung. He hung on for about three miles before he eventually caught the branches of a cottonwood near the bank and climbed the tree to seek refuge. I guess that was his lucky day!

Total damage was over two billion, (in today's dollars, over 8.9 billion). Willford, Sugar City, Rexburg and Hibbard were the hardest hit towns.

The National Guard was called out and disaster plans were in the making. All available state policemen were being summoned to help with the situation.

Doug needed to pack his things immediately and report. He had no idea how long he would be gone, or what the conditions were where he would be helping people.

Phone service wasn't what it is today. He would only be able to contact me via relay through the state police, or through landlines that may or may not be available. There were no cell phones, computers, or internet back then.

It was a worrisome time, not only because I could only imagine what Doug was doing or seeing, but because we had no idea what the repercussions were going to be for citizens of that part of Idaho. Property loss to thousands was unimaginable and just how were these historical old towns ever going to recover?

Recover, they did. The Teton Dam originally cost forty eight million dollars to build. It was never rebuilt. In 2016 on its 40th anniversary, The Teton Dam disaster was touted by the Idaho Statesman as being "the worst man-made disaster in Idaho history".

21

Fish in the Well

I found an ad in the paper one day advertising a little pony for sale. I always wanted a horse. We now owned enough land to have one. The pony wasn't very tall, but he was tall enough for me at five foot three.

We called the girl advertising him and went to check him out. She rode Chico in 4-H. He was used in play-days, bareback riding as well as saddle, and was pretty easy going. I climbed on him and tried him out. I liked his spunky, yet kind disposition. The girl rode him over to our house. We put up a little corral for him, and constructed a three way shed. We were now the owners of our first horse!

Chico was great fun. I would climb on his back, pull out little boy up behind me, then pull our daughter up in front of me. We rode bareback. We rode all over the trails on the BLM land in the back. We rode down the road to Alexander Subdivision, our old neighborhood, about a mile away from where we lived. I would call our friends, the Chandlers, who's home include a place to "park" the pony. She would put the coffee on. I would load the kids up and away we would go.

Many of the younger children in the neighborhood were

born about the same time as our children. They enjoyed playing with each other while we mothers visited. I was glad we still lived so close. Many times our little girl would fall asleep on the ride down. Sometimes she would lose her little cowboy boots on the way. I would stop off on the way home and pick them up off the side of road.

We didn't always stay on Chico. He was a real gentleman while we were on the road, but when we went off into the desert, he sometimes decided he wanted to act up. If something looked a little off to him, or if the kids happened to hit him with their foot in the wrong spot, he would bump up with a soft buck. Our little boy would fall off one side while our little girl and I tumbled off the other. We were always lucky and never hit any wayward rocks. Usually everyone was laughing while the pony just stood there with a big grin on his face. We would load back on and continue on our way.

Sometimes on our way home, we would stop at the bottom of the property where water always stood in big puddles for Chico to have a well deserved drink. The water ran off our neighbor's property from irrigation of his fruit trees.

I though he must have a massive well to be able to freely water so many fruit trees and let the water run down along our road and into the ditch.

Then, our little boy showed me some little baby fish in the ditch in the water. He got a stick and pretended he was fishing and catching them. This was extremely interesting. Not only did the neighbor have an unending supply of water from his well, it also provided fish!

A few days later, we rode Chico down the road to the far end of the subdivision. There at cul-de-sac, our neighbor's property jutted against the curve of the irrigation canal that fed tilled fields in the valley below. I guess he didn't have a magic well after all!

I decided to make use of the wasted water running along our road and put trimmings of willow and Russian olive trees into the ground to see if they would root and I could start trees.

A while after we moved, someone else must have figured out where the farmer was getting his extra water. The orchard of fruit trees no longer exists. Amazingly, many of the tree branches I planted took root and continued to grow. To this day, beautiful shade trees line the lane of the place we used to call home.

We were fortunate this spring to catch the present owner of our ten-acre house at home. They also have two young children about the age our children were when we owned the place. Surprisingly, they were just beginning a major kitchen remodel. She invited us in and we were able, for one last time, see the kitchen as we made it. I stood by the sliding glass doors and looked at the same patio where the bull snake napped in the sun under our little son's tricycle. She was amazed by the story. Evidently the bull snakes have found other digs. She said she rarely sees snakes. I'm thankful that another young family can enjoy our desert home.

22

A Job I Never Planned

That August I started working at the Elmore County Law Enforcement Center. I was pretty busy with life at home, but there was irrigation pipe we wanted to purchase, and a field to plant, more fencing was needed, the list went on with improvements we could think of, but our budget just stretched so far. When we needed to haul things, we used a small flatbed trailer Doug had for his snowmobile. We really needed a pickup.

A secretarial job came available at the law enforcement building in Mountain Home and I applied.

Child care worked out great, because the job was evening shifts, so as long as Doug was on day shifts, we just traded places being at home with the children. I had weekends off, so on his three day weekends, we had two days off together.

When he worked nights, I would drop the kids off at the house of a nice older couple who would put them down to bed. I would pick them up when I got off about midnight.

A few weeks later, one of the police dispatchers quit. I was called in to the dispatch room. They asked me to sit at the radio and showed me how to use it. I answered a few calls, and was shown how to use the 10-code and the phonetic alphabet (hometown police versus government service). They showed me how to send out a NCIC (National Crimes Information Center) teletype. They asked me to read some information to officers over the radio. It was all very interesting. I was wondering why they showed me all of this.

The next day I was called to the police chief's office. He asked me how I would feel if he changed my job to dispatching. He also asked how I would feel dispatching at times to my husband, because sometimes, depending on the location of the State Police officer, they might not be able to reach the State Police channel. In that case, they needed to go through local police channels. I could end up dispatching during an emergency to my husband. How would that affect me?

I responded that although I was a bit intimidated by the idea, I was interested in all of the different functions of a dispatcher. I also stated that I thought that I would be okay in an emergency situation, even if my husband was involved. I stated that we had a good working relationship and respect for each other and that I possessed confidence in my husband's ability to perform his duty and the best thing I could do was perform mine if the situation arose.

I was then trained as a police dispatcher/matron. I was issued a uniform. The job was both interesting and challenging. Dispatcher communications have changed immensely over the years. In 1976, the call center was outfitted with a radio with several channels, including Mountain Home Sheriff, Owyhee County Sheriff, Mountain Home MAST Helicopter Program (lifesaving emergency rescue airlift), Idaho State Police, Mountain Home Fire Department, and Mountain Home Ambulance. There was also CB communication.

We also answered and sent out NCIC information on stolen items such as cars and guns, or wanted individuals. We checked license plates or stolen guns frequently for the officers through this database.

On weekends there were two girls on the evening shift. On weekdays, there was only one. Our shifts rotated, but we never needed to rotate to the midnight shift, because there was one lady that only wanted that shift. It still worked out pretty well with the children. I didn't like being away from them during the day, but the shifts changed often enough that it never was that long of a period.

I got a large fish tank at home. When I would come home after a really busy day at work, I would stare at the fish in the fish tank until my eyes started to close. Then I could finally go to sleep.

You become hardened to some things. You still care as much, but either you survive work like that or you don't. The only way to survive it is to know when you have done the very best anyone could do. Then you know whatever happens is not in your hands anymore. I learned that the first time there was a call on someone that rear-ended a truck on a motorcycle.

I called the police officers. I called the ambulance. I did all I could do.

The true answer to the question the Chief asked me when I was hired to dispatch, "How do you think you would react if you had to dispatch to your husband in an emergency situation?" came one day unexpectedly.

Doug was patrolling State Highway 78 by Grandview. He called in an out of state license plate. His transmission was pretty broken, which wasn't surprising, given where he was. He was calling us because he hadn't been able to contact the Idaho State Police channel in the area he was in.

I ran the license plate and it came back a hit. I got back on the radio to raise Doug to advise him it was a hit, but could not get an answer, only static. I called the Owyhee County Sheriff on his channel and advised him of Doug's location and the information on the hit. Thankfully, he was not far away.

Right afterward, Doug broke through on the radio. I gave him the information. The radio started breaking up so I never got a confirmation. All we could do was wait. A few minutes later the Owyhee County Sheriff came back on to report a prisoner was in custody and that they would be in transport.

23

Off to School

One morning in the early spring of 1977 we woke slowly since we both arrived home late after an evening shift. It had been a long week for the both of us. His three day weekend was here. It was my weekend off.

As I was fixing breakfast, Doug announced that he decided he should quit the State Police and go back to school.

The suggestion came out of nowhere and hit me like a truck at full speed. I thought our lives had settled into some sort of routine, however hard it was at times jockeying child care between two shift jobs, we made it work. We lived in a nice home and were fortunate to have many good friends.

His argument was that he couldn't see himself driving the road and doing accident investigation work for the rest of his career. He felt he needed to get out of shift work.

He felt that his best chance of doing what he wanted to do was to go back to school. When asked what he wanted to do in school. He explained that he would finish his degree in school administration and become a school principal.

I told him I was tired of moving and I would have to think about it. It sounded like an idea that might die with the weekend.

It did not.

Our home went on the market in March of 1977. We kept five acres of land and sold five acres and the home for about $80,000.

I told Doug that he could go back to school, but I was going to school too.

We both enrolled at the University of Idaho for summer classes and rented student housing. School would start the first part of June.

Our old neighbors near our brick house, the Chandlers, retired from the Air Force and moved to Phoenix Arizona the fall of 1976. They were trying to talk us into visiting them.

After we closed on the house toward the end of May, we decided to take a family trip to visit the Chandlers and see a piece of the Southwest before starting school. That vacation still stands out as one of the classics in family memories. As young as the children were, they still have memories of the blooming cacti, the Grand

Canyon, the red rocks and of getting to swim and play with their old friends.

When we got back we said goodbye to our home in Mountain Home, but not to our friends.

We still return to see a rich desert where our homes with the trees and bushes we planted continue to thrive and make adventures for young families.

The desert soil is rich and grows many things including old friendships that were started there, took root and have continued to flourish along with our memories.

We spent seven years in Mountain Home, Idaho, from the spring of 1970 through the spring of 1977.

24

Moscow Here We Come

Moscow, Idaho, (pronounced Mossko with the o pronounced long, Not MosCOW, like town with the same spelling in Russia) is situated on the Palouse country in the southern part of the northern Idaho panhandle.

The University of Idaho is the oldest University in the State of Idaho. In 1862 The Morrill Act granted eligible states 30,000 acres of land to establish institutes of learning that would focus on fields such as agriculture, science, military science and engineering. Governor Stevenson signed the Territorial Legislature's Council Bill Number 20, thus creating the University of Idaho as a land grant university on January 30, 1889. The fact that the University of Idaho is a land grant university makes it more affordable.

People in the southern part of the state still make comments that they don't know why the University was placed in such an out-of-the way location. Growing up in the northern panhandle of Idaho, I always thought it was a perfect location!

A couple of interesting historical happenings played into why Moscow was chosen as the site for a University. It is said that it was chosen as sort of an olive branch to the citizens of the northern part of the state.

The first hard feelings between North Idaho and South Idaho, if you want to divide it as such, were caused when the state capitol was moved from Lewiston to Boise in December of 1864, about a year after it became a state.

The second rift was when Congress voted to sever North Idaho from South Idaho and attach it to Washington State, but President Grover Cleveland pocket vetoed the bill in 1887.

The University's first classes began October 3, 1892. The first class consisted of 40 students, and the first graduating class, which was in 1896, consisted of four graduates, two men and two women.

The University now has an active enrollment of over 13,000 students, with well over 11,000 of those students living on the Moscow campus. Many of the students hail from Idaho and have parents, grandparents and great grandparents who attended. It has satellite locations throughout the state, and online classes available making it easier for everyone to attend.

Moscow, Idaho is the headquarters for the Appaloosa Horse Registry. The Appaloosa was named the official state horse in 1975. It is said that the Nez Perce people of the Palouse developed this original American horse breed. The Appaloosa breed was nearly wiped out during the Nez Perce war of 1877.

The Palouse country around Moscow is the largest lentil growing area in the United States. Other crops grown in the region are spring and winter wheat, barley, peas, garbanzos, bluegrass, cereal grains, rape and mustard.

By the middle of May, 1977, we were moved in to student housing at the University of Idaho. The houses were several units of 4-plexes. I called them double-decker. Unless you were an end unit, you ended up with someone on either side of you, but you had two stories of house. There was a nice park area for the children, plus lots of walking around the park-like campus.

We were not able to keep our dog, Jessie with us, but I refused to give her up, so she stayed on a farm with an old friend in Osburn, Idaho.

While Doug and I attended classes, the children attended the campus daycare. That daycare was run by students majoring in education. The kids really received great care and got to take frequent field trips around the campus. I even saw them all getting ice cream from the ice cream truck one day.

We spent our weekends learning the surrounding area. Doug received his teaching degree at the University of Idaho, so he was familiar with the Moscow campus, but didn't really spend much time learning much about the area other than where the best bars and pizza houses were.

I was taking art and English classes. I loved to explore the countryside looking for old barns to take pictures of and paint for class.

The summer semester passed all too quickly. We both did well in our classes and the children settled happily into the new routine.

I really missed and worried about our dog. Jessie tried to run away from the farm where she was being kept. She now needed to be tied when she was out of doors alone. When school broke between summer and fall classes, we decided to find housing in the countryside.

We found a two bedroom furnished trailer for sale in a mobile home court outside of Moscow, but fairly close to the college. We purchased it and moved in the next weekend. I was overjoyed. We could have our family dog with us again! It also felt great to be out in the country.

It was good to have her for company, because Doug

decided to work at the U.S. Forest Service in Silverton, Idaho during the break between summer and fall classes.

That meant that I would stay in Moscow in the trailer in the countryside with our children, and he would board at the Forest Service Building in Silverton, Idaho.

25

Just Around the Corner from the Poor Farm

In my first book, I described my life in our hometown of Wallace, Idaho. We lived around the corner from the bedroom community of Silverton. My dad used to say that we lived "just around the corner from the poor farm," with the double meaning that the actual first poor farm in the State of Idaho was just around the corner from us in Silverton; also meaning that with seven children, my parents always lived "close to the budget."

It might seem strange that I say that Doug "boarded" at the U.S. Forest Service Building in Silverton, for the month break from school, but that was a special building. It was set up with bedrooms and a very large kitchen in addition to the administrative offices needed for regular U.S.F.S. business.

It already possessed a rich history by the time the U.S. Forest Service acquired it as its headquarters for the Wallace District of the Coeur d'Alene National Forest.

The building was the main structure of the state of Idaho's first poor farm back in the late 1800s.

The very first session of the Idaho Territorial Legislature in 1863 assigned the legal responsibility of caring for the poor to its county commissioners.

Poorhouses were planned to be well run, cost effective ways to provide assistance to the poor. Four Idaho counties were originally given the authority to create poor farms, the first of which was Shoshone County. Some of the other counties that eventually had poor farms were Ada County, Twin Falls County, Idaho County and Bonner County.

People that lived on poor farms originally worked there to repay their debt to society. Residents that were able to work would put up fruit, raised chickens, milk cows, cattle and swine, grew vegetables and grain, and generally provided for the residents.

As time passed, poorhouses became primarily, nursing homes for impoverished elderly people.

The Shoshone county poor farm was built in 1894. It consisted of much of the Silverton, Idaho area. It included pasture, a large gardening area, a large barn and several outbuildings and the large main institutional building.

The barn and outbuildings gradually disappeared starting in the late 1940s into the 1950s as Silverton became a bedroom community to Wallace.

An "Opportunity School" for children that might have problems with learning the conventional way was run into the early 1960s on the property.

The main building became the Shoshone County Nursing home officially about 1960 and continued operation until about 1975.

The U.S. Forest Service began operation in the building about 1976.

26

The Circular Trail to the Future

That one month, from the middle of July to the middle of August, when school would start up again, flew by. I kept busy painting and going for picnic hikes with the kids and dog, making one weekend trip to Wallace to see Doug and my family.

I was excited about school starting again. Our little boy was ready to start kindergarten. Our baby girl loved the University daycare and was already able to ask about the caregivers she liked and was excited about seeing again.

Fall was upon us, Doug returned with news that he was having second thoughts continuing with getting his Masters degree. He had two semesters left to go to get his degree, but he explained that he had some time to think while he was away and found the same questions haunting him. Did he really want to be a principal? Was education the path he was really meant to follow?

We realized early on that our savings would only carry us so far. At some point, we were going to have to look at the reality of getting a part time job while going to school. The reality just hit earlier than later. This was the reason Doug spent the last month working for the Forest Service.

He confessed that he called his former supervisors in Boise while he was staying in Silverton. He was offered a job if he returned. He felt confident that he was meant for a career path dealing with some facet of government. He was determined to return to Boise and the State Police.

I was, well, basically numb. Everyone goes through hard times in marriages. This was definitely one of those times. I didn't know where to turn.

I could, either, stay where I was with the kids, get a part time job and put in for student loans and let Doug go back if he wanted to, or go with Doug and let the cards fall where they might.

I chose the latter.

We sold our trailer to some students moving in to go to school and back to Boise we went.

27

Pasadena in Boise

Doug's parents were happy to see us back in Boise. They moved from northern Idaho specifically to be closer to us after our son was born in 1972.

They were supportive, but disappointed when we migrated to Moscow. They were overjoyed to welcome us back closer to them so they could enjoy more of the grandchildren.

I'm not sure how overjoyed they were to have us living with them temporarily, but they never complained.

Doug started work almost immediately dispatching in the headquarters of the Idaho State Police. He was told he would receive a patrol assignment as soon as one became available.

We found a home on Pasadena drive on the south bench off Overland road in Boise. We moved in about two weeks before school started.

Our son began kindergarten at Owyhee elementary. I thought he was getting so old! He wouldn't even turn six years old until later in the month of September and he couldn't wait to start reading. He wanted to ride his bicycle to school, so I would follow him in the car the roughly ten blocks to school, and come back when he got out and do the same thing. I did this not all days, but once in a while so he could practice. Most days I just drove him and picked him up.

Things have a way of working out if you give them a chance. We were settled, busy and happy with our life again.

University life was a good learning experience, but life with the daily routine and grandparents close was quite fine. The neighbors on either side of us became good friends. On one side lived a couple with grown children. They were great to visit with casually. On the other side lived a couple with the children the same age as ours. They were fun for outings with the children. They also owned a dog similar to ours. We would go on family hikes and sleigh riding together with the kids in the winter.

Six months passed incredibly fast. Six months was how long we lived in our home on Pasadena Street. It too was to become one of many homes to be added to our list of memories with a street name or town to mark the spot where a piece of us remains. The handy thing is that it is easier to keep track of the years when they are marked with spots, those spots with memories.

Doug came home from work one day in early June of

1978. He was to get a patrol position in Fruitland, Idaho. The change would take effect the first of July.

We sold our home and moved to our new home in Fruitland, Idaho the first part of July.

We now owned a split level home across the street from overlooking the Snake River, on the Idaho / Oregon border in Fruitland, Idaho.

28

Fruitland Idaho and the Payette Valley

There are so many parts of Idaho to love. When we eventually left the Payette Valley, I made Doug promise, as I have other times, that we would return to this area to live the rest of our lives. We are going to have to live a lot of lives!

As long as we are talking about the Payette Valley, I am going to take you on a chapter-long tour of the entire Payette Valley. I am getting ahead of myself for part of it, because in 1978, Doug and I actually, only explored the lower portion of the Valley from New Plymouth to Fruitland, but later…..well, we will get to that later. Anyway, eventually, you will see why you get the whole tour.

The Payette Valley runs north and west of Boise roughly 40 miles along the Payette River from the foothills and pines of the Boise National Forest and Black Canyon Dam to the farm fields and high banks of the Snake River where it divides Idaho and Oregon. The Payette River was named after Francois Payette. Francois was born in Canada in 1793. He was a fur trader and explorer and spent a great amount of time exploring the Payette River basin area with Donald McKenzie and other mountain men from about 1818. He was one of the first white men to settle in southwestern Idaho. He was inducted into the Idaho Hall of Fame in 1998, according to the Argus Observer.

Fruitland is at the far westerly end of the Valley.

This friendly agricultural town with fertile sandy loam soil and a mild, temperate climate became a popular fruit growing area for farmers when the area was first settled back in the late 1800s.

Fruitland was part of John Hall's original 160 acres homesteaded in 1897. B.F. Tussing, who owned a packing shed one quarter mile south of the present Fruitland, is credited with naming the town.

In 1906 the Payette Valley Railroad began shipping apples from a local packing house. Over the next few years more packing houses were added as shippers. The town grew toward the railroad shipping site of Buckingham Station, two miles east of the present town site. Hundreds of acres of sweet apples of many varieties were and still are grown in fields around Fruitland, packed in local packing houses and shipped all over the United States and the world.

In 1978, about 2500 people lived in Fruitland. Today, that population has doubled.

While continuing to be an agricultural area, Fruitland has also become a bedroom community to larger towns such as Nampa and Caldwell.

A partner town to Fruitland, Payette, Idaho, lies a little over 5 miles away, just across the Payette River to the north. Payette is the county seat for Payette County and boasts a population of about 7500 people.

Following the Payette River to the east about seven and a half miles will find you in the quiet little farming town of New Plymouth (population about 1700). The New Plymouth area is surrounded by many acres of tilled fields in the spring. Farmers grow crops from kidney and lima beans and corn to alfalfa and mint.

Further up the Valley in a northeasterly direction, is the town of Emmett. Emmett is the most westerly town and the county seat of Gem County, (dubbed the "Gem of the Payette").

Emmett is also popular for a very mild but temperate climate. Even though it is further north than Fruitland and Payette, It is tucked in between foothills separating it from the Boise Valley, and the foothills of the Boise National forest. Squaw Butte, at 5,906 feet, stands as a silent soldier behind Emmett to the northeast. Squaw Butte was named by Native Americans. They used the Emmett area as their winter retreat.

Emmett, Idaho was originally called "Emmettville." Tom Calahan was an early settler, who homesteaded 160 acres in the area in the fall of 1863. In 1868, Tom Calahan was appointed postmaster and a small building was moved to his ranch. It was decided to name the area Emmettville, after Tom's young son, Emmett. Later, the post office was moved but kept the name, Emmettville. A couple of years later, the "ville" part later was removed to become simply Emmett. In 1883 James Wardwell had the town platted, and in 1900 the town was incorporated as Emmett. Later, in March 1902, the Idaho Northern railroad came into the valley.

The arrival of the railroad, and two more events helped Emmett to grow and prosper through the early 2000s.

One of these events was the building of Black Canyon Dam. It was constructed just to the northeast of Emmett on the Payette River. Canal systems brought irrigation water to the Payette Valley enabling farmers to expand their orchards to grow fruit to export throughout the country by way of the rail system.

Another boon for Emmett arrived in the form of lumber. The Boise Payette Company opened a new lumber mill in Emmett, Idaho in 1913. In 1957, the Boise Payette Company became the Boise Cascade Company. During Boise Cascade's tenure in Emmett, it also opened a plant to build homes. That plant was in operation until 2001.

After operating for 98 years, the Boise Cascade Sawmill closed in Emmett in 2011.

In 2017, 34 acres of Boise Cascade mill land was gifted to the Idaho Foundation for Parks and Lands.

In 1978, Emmett was a thriving fruit growing town with a busy lumber industry. Train whistles echoed down the valley as loads of fruit and lumber left for points around the world. The population in 1978 was about 4,500. Today, despite changes, it is a city of just under 7,000 people.

Housing developments have replaced most of the orchards. Where multicolored blooming fruit trees canvassed the Valley in the 1900s, now homes now dot the landscape. Families move here with the promise of larger yards, and close proximity to Black Canyon Dam, its man-made lake and picnic areas and a town with a laid back atmosphere of yesteryear. The trade-off is a commute of roughly twenty-five miles to jobs in Boise, Nampa or Caldwell.

Further up the Payette above Black Canyon Dam lie the picturesque small farm towns of Moutour, Sweet and Ola.

Montour lies directly along the banks of the Payette. According to the Gem County Historical Society,

Montour actually existed as a home for peoples as early as 5,000 years ago. Archeological digs in the area have uncovered evidence of native dwellings for people using it possibly as a winter home.

Gem County Historical Museum reports that Montour was originally called Marsh.

In 1867, Edson Marsh hired out as a farmhand at a ranch near the present town of Montour. Marsh eventually bought half interest in the ranch for $2500. In 1870 a post office was established on the ranch. In 1871 it was decided to refer to the area as Squaw Creek. In 1877, Marsh was named postmaster and in June of 1889, the area was renamed Marsh.

In 1912, a man by the name of William Dewey Jr. was in charge of building the Idaho Northern railroad up the Payette River from Emmett to McCall. They purchased the land the Marsh post office was on.

It is said that the railroad company platted the town and Dewey's secretary suggested the name of Montour. Montour is a French word which means "setting" or "frame". It is said she chose the word because Montour is in a beautiful setting, like a picture in a frame.

Montour still is a beautiful setting. Much of the area is managed by the Idaho Fish and Game as a Wildlife

Management area. There is no longer a post office, but the inhabitants are friendly and proud of their little slice of paradise.

The same can be said of Sweet, and all 554 people who inhabit the town. It is just up the road northwest of Montour. When you see Sweet, you will know why someone named it just that, Sweet. It is. Even today, if you ask me where to go for a picnic and views, I might suggest Sweet. Today, Sweet elementary school has around 36 students from kindergarten to fifth grade.

A small red building with a porch proudly displays the sign "Sweet, Idaho Post Office 83670." Flowers bloom in the window planter.

No rushing traffic, no traffic lights. If you unroll your car window, you will probably hear a meadow lark or a cow mooing.

The tiny town of Ola is what I call, "at the top of the hill." It is 15.22 miles north of Sweet. Ola also has its own post office, originally established in 1875 by Carroll Baird, a homesteader in the area. In 1882, the post office building along Squaw Creek was replaced by moving it to the General Store. Carroll Baird chose the name of Ola, meaning in Swede, "an old Swede that happened along."

Before the post office was established, mail used to be delivered by pack horses and snowshoes in the winter along a trail followed by the Umatilla Indians in Oregon to reach council grounds in Idaho on the Weiser River. The trail was later named the Brownlee Trail by miners who also followed the shortcut from the Boise Basin to the Brownlee Ferry on the Idaho Oregon border and into Oregon by way of current Council, Idaho and Brownlee Dam reservoir. The trail wound from Harris Creek below Horseshoe Bend north and west across the mountains, Payette Valley and the Weiser River Valley. You can still follow portions of the trail. Check mostly dirt road signs that say Brownlee Road. It will take you on some interesting adventures.

Ola attaches to the Payette Valley by way of Squaw Creek that tumbles down from Squaw Butte foothills through Sweet and into the Payette. For this reason, it is also considered to be in the Upper Squaw Creek Valley, with Sweet being in the lower Squaw Creek Valley.

 It takes about thirty-six minutes to drive to Ola from Sweet, as it is a quiet two lane winding country road. Don't be in any hurry. Enjoy the view!

If you drop down the hill on a dirt road (Brownlee Road, part of the old Brownlee Trail), northeast of Ola about 19 miles (about a 32 minute drive), you will end up in the lovely little hamlet of Gardena, Idaho, population about twenty people.

Gardena sits in the sunshine, each home with a tidy lawn and blooming trees in the spring looking out at the Payette River flowing by. A picturesque steel bridge across the Payette will take you either north up State Highway 55 to Smith's Ferry, Cascade and McCall, or south back to Horseshoe Bend, about 5 miles downstream on State Highway 55.

Horseshoe Bend is the last incorporated city in the Payette Valley. It was the first town I remember considering as being truly in South Idaho on my first trip down from North Idaho so many years ago, when we were transferred to Mountain Home, Idaho.

When Doug and I arrived in Horseshoe Bend, all I saw were dry foothills. Although there was a beautiful river snaking its way through the town in the form of a gigantic horseshoe, all I saw were brown hills with no trees, only sparse brush. All I felt was a dry heat I was unaccustomed to and the glare of an all too bright sun.

My first thought was that we had been sentenced to Hell.

I now feel guilty for such thoughts. After becoming acclimatized to a dryer climate, and having hiked in more desert like terrain, I realize that Horseshoe Bend is a beautiful town by any standards certain times of the year, and a small town, just like so many busy little logging/agricultural/tourist 'bergs with the face of hardworking people just trying to make a living and enjoying a piece of small town life. Horseshoe Bend is in Boise County. Today the population is about 765 people. Boise County's population is about 7,830.

It is a town full of mining, logging and railroad history if you just take the time to listen to the citizens and do some adventurous investigating.

When gold was discovered in the Boise Basin in 1862, Horseshoe Bend, (Warrinersville by name, at that time, named after a local sawmill owner) was basically the gateway and staging area to the popular gold fields in the mountains to the east of the town. Many of the miners, businessmen and gamblers who followed in their wake made their way from California by way of Oregon and the Brownlee Trail.

After 1867 the name of the town was changed to Horseshoe Bend because of the horseshoe shape the Payette River makes as it winds its way through town.

Others came by way of a trail forged by Tim Goodale in 1862. After following the same old Indian trails through Oregon, he cut off at Brownlee Ferry on the Snake River and followed the river south to Parma, Idaho to Martin's

Landing. From there, he followed the Boise River west, thereafter, veering north to Emmett, descending a steep ridge approximately two miles west of the current State Highway 16. He led prospective gold seekers and merchants on their way to seek their fortunes in the Boise Basin on up the Payette River into Horseshoe Bend, and from there up Harris Creek road to the gold fields beyond.

In 1863 a toll road was established by five men, Thomas Reeves, Felix Harris, Tom Pettingill, Hank Hawkins and Phillip Fry. The toll road ran from Placerville (Harris Creek road) to a spot called Pickett Corral Hill. Pickett's Corral was itself a notorious spot. For a couple of years at the beginning of the gold rush, travelers, miners and farmers were troubled by a band of horse thieves headquartered at a spot on the bluff just north of Emmett on the road to Horseshoe Bend above and on the east side of Black Canyon Dam. (The old toll gate road followed on the south side of the Payette River from Emmett to Horseshoe Bend). In 1864, vigilantes drove out the Pickett Corral gang.

Placerville, Pioneerville, Centerville, Grimes Creek and Idaho City sprung up and exploded almost overnight with gold hungry fortune seekers. In 1863, the population of the entire Boise Basin was said to have been estimated at between 25,000 and 70,000 people.

By 1864, Idaho City was the largest city in the Northwest.

After the gold rush, things quieted down for the area. Horseshoe Bend became a quiet logging, farming and railroad town.

In 1998, the Boise Cascade Mill, and principle industry for the town, closed. Horseshoe Bend is now primarily a bedroom community to the Boise Valley and tourist gateway to the Boise and Payette National Forests and upper Payette River drainage.

29

A Little about the North Fork of the Payette River

McCall, Idaho lies just south of the 45th parallel and almost directly in the center of the state north to south.

 I am going to skip ahead a few years in time, since we never actually got to know McCall until the late 1980s. It was an unplanned visit, but since we are talking about the Payette, I felt the story belonged here.

McCall has been close to my heart ever since I rushed our older son from 4-H camp to the closest hospital in the area which was in McCall for an emergency appendectomy in the late 1980s. We spent a scary few nights at a lodge in this pristine mountain town and ended up falling in love. Over the ensuing years, this town has been our savior for entertaining teens with too much energy. The winter snows are the best for skiing. In the summer, the mountain hikes, boating and swimming in the lakes might end with fish to cook over evening campfires, ghost stories and huckleberries picked from nearby bushes for desert. It can put even the wildest teenager in a better mood.

The north fork of the Payette River starts north of

McCall, Idaho. It flows into Payette Lake, then southward past Lake Fork, Donnelly and into Lake Cascade (formerly Cascade Reservoir, a man-made reservoir). Continuing south through Long Valley and Smith's Ferry, it joins with the South Fork to become the Payette River at Banks, Idaho.

Francois Payette, for whom the river is named, (and as I mentioned earlier in the book) was a French-Canadian fur trapper who worked for the North West Company and was one of the first people of European descent to explore the Payette River basin. According to the Payette County website, Francois Payette was a Canadian canoe-man and fur trapper. In 1810 at 18 years of age, he was hired by John Jacob Astor of the Pacific Fur Company. In 1812 he joined other trappers who traveled to the mouth of the Columbia by ship and built Fort Astoria. Six years later, in 1818, Payette, along with Donald McKenzie, explored and trapped what later was named the Payette River Basin. Interestingly, another man named Jack Weiser was in that same exploratory party. The Weiser River and the city of Weiser is named after him.

McCall, Idaho was named for Tom McCall, who homesteaded in the area around 1891 and became one of the town leaders. McCall was a lively town back in the day, full of fur trappers, loggers, miners, bars, dance halls and houses of ill repute. It has been said that firearms were still allowed in bars into the 1980s.

McCall has been home to an annual Winter Carnival since 1924. This small, astoundingly beautiful mountain town draws upwards of fifty-thousand visitors during the carnival. The Ice Sculpture contest is one of the favorite activities, as is the annual dog sled race.

After retirement, Doug and I owned a dog sled and three dogs. We never ran in the race, but certainly enjoyed dog sledding in McCall, Cascade and Smith's Ferry as a recreation.

My favorite place of all in McCall is Ponderosa State Park. I love to hike the trails to the overlook at the top. The view overlooking crystal clear waters on an early fall afternoon will take your breath away.

30

What about the South Fork and the Middle Fork?

The Payette would not be the river it is without the South Fork and the Middle Fork.

The South Fork of the Payette's roots lie on the west side of the Sawtooth Wilderness under Mount Payette. Mount Payette stands at 10,211 feet. The South Fork then follows a path down past Grandjean to Lowman on State Highway 21. From that point it takes a southwesterly direction into Garden Valley where it meets with its brother, the Middle Fork just outside of the friendly mountain metropolis of Crouch. Together, they head for Banks, Idaho to join with the North Fork of the Payette, dancing onward towards Gardena and Horseshoe Bend.

Grandjean, Idaho was named for Emile Grandjean, an immigrant that came to Idaho before it was a state. In 1890 he settled on Grandjean Peak and built himself a log cabin. The site later became the Grandjean Ranger Station. He came to mine, hunt and trap, but because of his studies in forestry in Denmark, he was hired as a forester where he served in the Boise National Forest from 1906 to 1922. This information is listed on roadside marker #435 on Idaho State Highway 21.

If you ever want to see the power of a snow slide, take a drive on a sunny day in late spring to view the marks of winter in the high mountains. The Grandjean area is famous for snow slides. State Highway 21 regularly closes in the winter from snow slides. You can view the chutes on the mountainsides along the highway with downed trees and see marks on the banks and snow poles where the snow has covered the road with sometimes as much as 50 feet of snow, rocks and debris.

Grandjean sits at an elevation of 5,400 feet and is in Custer County. It is famous for hot water as well as cold snow. Sacajawea Hot Springs is a great place to visit.

Its neighbor, Lowman, elevation 3,800 feet, is in Boise County. Although Lowman Idaho is described as an "unincorporated rural census-designated place, it has its own one room school. The one room school still teaches grades kindergarten through the fifth grade. Students in middle school and high school are bused downriver to Garden Valley. It also has a store and gas station, a community church, a café, a lodge, a bar, 25 full time residents,(as of the 2018 census) and vacation cabins.

Lowman is the place and country to find hunting outfitters, hunting and fishing guides and trail rides into the Sawtooth Wilderness. The Southfork Lodge on the

South fork of the Payette is a great place to stay, or visit for an afternoon. They serve excellent meals.

Lowman also has beautiful scenery, cross country ski and hiking trails and a multitude of elk, deer and other wildlife waiting to have their picture taken on the right day.

Garden Valley was originally settled by fur trappers. Around about 1863 while the gold rush in the Boise Basin, just over the hill from the South Fork of the Payette, was in its throws, Garden Valley began to grow and flourish as farmers discovered the fertile soil on the banks of the sunny South Fork were prime for producing the needed supplies to feed the hungry miners. The area was aptly named Garden Valley. It became the 'bread basket' producer of meat, grains, dairy products and produce.

In 1904, a hydroelectric plant was built on the South Fork by Norman Gratz, his earthen dam failed, so he sold out to W.H. Estabrook, who thereafter built a 50 foot wooden dam on the South Fork with power line to serve dredges in the Boise Basin.

Extensive commercial logging began in earnest along the South Fork during the 1930s. Sawmills were a common site in the area into the 1950s.

Garden Valley, formally listed as an unincorporated census designated area and the town of Crouch, incorporated in the 1950s, and on the Middle Fork, continue to be popular vacation spots. It has also been home to many families for generations.

The area boasts greenhouses that help supply Treasure Valley retailers, exceptionally beautiful scenery with picture perfect mountain views, great fishing, abundant wildlife, numerous hot springs both developed and undeveloped, summer theatre, ATV rentals, cabin rentals and B&Bs, a golf course and resort, cross country ski and snowshoe trails, a snowmobile park, also whitewater rafting, a rodeo grounds, camping and RV spots.

Garden Valley contains several churches, the area post office, a local library, gas station and convenience store with a sandwich shop.

Garden Valley School District is an above average public school with over 268 students, grades K-12.

When you enter the city of Crouch, you think for a moment you have gone backwards in time to the old west. They still have a boardwalk, old time hardware where you can find anything from caulk to candy, mouse traps to molding, from nails to nuts to peanuts. If they don't have it, they will order it. The buildings are well kept with a rustic flavor. In the morning you can find your local coffee shop that will rival the best brand names. To satisfy the appetite, you can walk across the street for a quick lunch on the boardwalk or have the meal of a lifetime at the restaurant in the middle. If you feel like just browsing, there is the Center for the Arts featuring local artists, the local Merc, a variety store or the weekend flea market.

The grocery store is more than you would expect with a drugstore included. The town has its own medical clinic and physical therapist, gas station, and local radio station. Crouch has character. Garden Valley greets you with adventure and avenue. They are partners in a river basin of wilderness and wildlife.

31

Life in Fruitland in 1978

Our home in Fruitland was situated where we could easily walk down the road and across the street and overlook the Snake River as it winds its way towards the Columbia 100 miles west of Lewiston, Idaho and onward to the ocean.

With the kids, we put a message in a bottle and tossed it into the river to see if it would eventually make its way across the ocean.

Our home was built in the 1950s. It was a split level design with two small bedrooms upstairs, a living room, dining room combination, the kitchen and a bathroom. The downstairs consisted of a nice double sized family room with a fireplace, a large master bedroom, a large laundry room with second kitchen and a bath. The worry about the design was that the children's bedrooms were upstairs. We were downstairs. It was an open stairway design and we were right below them and the floors were wood, so noise carried, but it was still a worry.

Our son tended to walk in his sleep, or only be partially awake when he got up to go bathroom. This may have been the case one evening. It was late, but Doug was working night shift and I hadn't gone to bed yet. The doors were locked, but there was no safety latch above where the kids could reach. I was coming upstairs to check on the children when I saw someone walking past the stairway. It was our boy. He went straight to the front door and started opening it. Luckily, he fumbled with the door knob since it was locked. I got to the door in a flash just as a car sped by on the road outside. Like I said, either he was sleep-walking or just not awake enough to know he went the wrong way to the bathroom. I asked him where he was going. He seemed confused when he answered, "To the bathroom!"

I took him to the bathroom and to bed. I slept on the couch that night, watching the doors. The next day we got latches put high up on the doors.

Another thing that scares me more in retrospect, than it did at the time, was the fact that the Snake River was so close. Our son had a "best friend" that lived just across the street. They were going back and forth to each other's house all the time. Sometimes we would allow them to go down to the river if they asked permission. We would always follow up with warnings to watch for where the river cut under the bank, and not to get too close. They could both swim, but the Snake is pretty big for soon to be first graders. We were both young mothers, though, and our boys seemed so old!

Money spent fast. Moves always cost a lot more than you think they will. We moved a lot. I decided to start up a daycare. That way I could stay home with the kids, and still contribute to the budget.

The daycare was a roaring success. We couldn't have lived in a better location. A great many of the jobs in the area were at food processing and packing plants. Many of these were located over the river in Ontario. There was also a Coca Cola bottling plant about four blocks away from us on U.S. 30. Many of the parents worked shifts, but that worked for me since Doug also worked shifts.

I ended up with five regular children from two to six and two drop-ins, three and five. This was pretty cool. Playmates for our children and a big family like I was used to! There were no daycare regulations at the time, so I don't know how the government would look at it, but it worked wonderfully. Some of the children were what you would call "special needs" now, but I really didn't give it a second thought. One that was two years old was fitted with a pacemaker. I remember you could feel it in the child's chest about the size, of a stuffed animal music box. This child was a little trooper, though, and joined in play with the others, never complaining. One child was three, but still was having trouble with potty training, and couldn't talk much. It was easy with that child being around the others. The transformation was miraculous. Soon the child was talking in small sentences. When the mother found out the child also was going to the bathroom regularly as well as talking with the other children, she cried.

I still have great memories of the children and their parents. Besides watching them all laugh and play together, one of the best memories was when Doug and I took them grocery shopping. We would sometimes do this when we needed groceries, Doug was home to help and we just were taking care of our four regular children plus our two. We had it down to a routine. We would get three grocery carts. The smaller four would sit in two of the carts. The larger two would help push the cart for groceries while we guided them. An older couple came in the store as were loading the children in the carts. The lady walked over to me and said, "Mum, are all of these children yours?"

I responded, "Yep, they sure are!"

Well, they were, for the moment!

That summer, we installed a four foot round pool in the back yard. Our son was already swimming when we left Mountain Home. We wanted our little daughter to learn before she got much older. In no time, both children were swimming like fish. Our friend's children enjoyed it also. We did not use it during daycare time. The ladder was put up and it was too tall for the children to climb. I kept a close eye on them in any case.

We owned just under an acre. The back was fenced and there was a small shed. I decided that besides my vegetable garden, we should do a little farming. We bought a couple of milking nanny goats.

Our daughter suffered from milk allergies and the goat's milk worked great. I set about learning how to make cottage cheese. Doug loves cottage cheese. This really pleased him. It turned out pretty good.

I learned how, since a goat is smaller than a cow, their milk will taste of what they eat a lot faster. If you stay with grass and alfalfa, their milk is very tasty. Another thing that affects the taste is the age of the goat. A young nanny has much sweeter milk than an old nanny. Different breeds of goats have different cream content and some people say they can tell the different taste of milk by the breed, but I guess I never became that much of an expert. My favorite is still the Saanen, with the Alpine taking a close second. We had one of each.

Next, I began making custard, puddings and custard pie. By fall, we had all of the baked goodies, whip cream, milk and cottage cheese that we could handle. The one thing I never perfected was actual cheese. I still wish I had.

Winter came early that year. The snow was deep, but it was fun taking the children sledding nearby and building snowmen and snow forts in the back yard. Fruitland grade school was a great little school. Our little boy felt right at home there in the first grade. He had a couple of friends and liked his teacher. The school year seemed like it was almost over before it started.

The nice thing about the Payette Valley is that when spring comes, the snow melts, and it dries up into the sandy loam soil quickly. Before you know it, fruit trees bloom, then the lilacs. Something is blooming from early spring till the heat of summer hits.

Before the heat of summer hit, we were planning our next move.

32

Idaho Falls Here We Come

Doug's early goal in his career as a State Police officer, after becoming an accident investigation expert, was to become a sergeant

When he came home from a visit at the District Office one day with a certain look on his face, I knew what was coming.

He was given a promotion to Sergeant. The promotion meant a move to the other side of the state. This was a side of the state I had never been to. Doug was somewhat familiar with the area, having spent time there during the Teton Dam disaster in 1976.

The move was hard, and yet it wasn't. There was no decision to make. The job was important. We were excited that he was offered the position.

The hard part was leaving all of our friends and leaving a really beautiful area of the state where we were very comfortable. The children enjoyed lots of playmates and our son finished his kindergarten school year here. He was excited about seeing his school friends again as a first grader.

Moving definitely gets harder as children grow older.

With that said, the spring of 1980 found us moving once more, to our brick home on Skyline Drive, Idaho Falls, Idaho.

Interest rates had risen quite profoundly. It is hard to picture it now, but the average interest rates on homes at that time were 11 percent or better. Our interest rate was 11 percent. We just felt lucky to have a comfortable home in a nice section of Idaho Falls.

 The rise in interest rates caused home sales to drop off dramatically. Our house in Fruitland sat on the market waiting for a buyer. With double house payments, our budget was stretched again. I soon got a part time job with Sears Credit. I was lucky that the job worked well with our daughter's kindergarten hours.

Life was a true adventure in Idaho Falls! The Tetons are beautiful! We spent much of the summer camping with our pickup and camper we purchased second hand from our neighbors on Pasadena in Boise. We loved that old Ford Pickup! We even named him Mr. Ed. The children and the dogs loved to hike and play in the mountains and go fishing. Well, mostly, the kids and dogs splashed while we tried to fish.

If you are ever up that way, check out the country around Victor (the largest city in Teton County with a population of around 2,000, and the county seat,

Driggs). You can't ask for more picturesque country. Wildlife abounds with plenty of places for fly fishing, or just plain 'against the tree fishing' on the Teton River.

While I am on the subject of places to check out, I feel I have to tell you another short story about a ghost town just 18 minutes away from the county seat of Driggs. It is the ghost town of Sam, Idaho. Sam has the unusual honor of being the home of Idaho's only coal mine, and one of two towns in Idaho named and started by the same man, Henry Floyd Samuels. The town of Sam was supported by a lucrative coal mine, the Teton Coal Company, for several years. It was lucrative enough to get the Oregon Short line to build a spur into the area for hauling out the coal produced. H.F. Samuels came to Idaho to practice law. Samuels, however, possessed multiple interests. He went on to became known as the father of the zinc industry in Idaho by patenting a more profitable process for extracting the mineral zinc from ore, which he put to use in his Success Mine and Milling operation. He was also co-owner in the Hercules Mine and Milling operation in Burke and Wallace. He eventually sold his shares of the Hercules, sold his zinc patent and built hotels, one in Wallace, Idaho and one in Spokane, Washington. They were both named 'The Samuels'. Samuels moved to a piece of land north of the beautiful town of Sandpoint, Idaho and Lake Pend O'reille, the fifth deepest lake in the United States.

Samuels built a ranch, complete with mansion, by the Great Northern tracks and raised registered cattle, shipping the beef on the railroad. A small community grew around the area and was named Samuels, Idaho. It is now marked by a gas station, convenience store and restaurant.

Besides our two children, our household still included our dog, Jessie, plus a new young yellow Labrador, Mandy. I bought Mandy as a pup the spring before from a farm in Ontario, Oregon that raised hunting dogs.

Mandy was a birthday present for Doug. I was excited to be in an area that was known for its multitude of pheasants, ducks and geese. I was hoping to get Doug hunting again as he had before we were married. I never hunted birds, but thought it would be fun. I liked to work with dogs and kept my promise to train Mandy. She had yet to retrieve a true duck, goose or pheasant, but we practiced a lot and she was very good at retrieving plenty of pretend ones.

The kids would help me with "game time" for the dogs in the back yard. We would get Jessie and Mandy to climb a five foot step ladder, and jump down. They would hunt for hidden items in the yard. When it came to retrieving things thrown, Mandy really excelled.

The Idaho Falls area also has great places to hunt

pheasant or waterfowl. Our neighbor really loved to hunt ducks. One day he was in his backyard watching Mandy. He didn't have a bird dog, so he asked if he could borrow her the next time he and his buddy went hunting. We let him.

When he came back, there were several ducks in the back of their pickup. Mandy was so excited about her trip, she kept jumping in the back of the pickup to pick up a duck and bring it to me. She went one more time with them that fall. That dog really loved to hunt!

That September, our son started the second grade at Skyline Elementary. Our daughter started kindergarten. They both enjoyed neighborhood friends and settled in quickly to a comfortable neighborhood life.

After only about three weeks working for Sears Credit, I was called by the College of Eastern Idaho about a job as a secretary. It was part time also, so I began work there the middle of October. I loved working at the college. I was actually able to use my shorthand that I learned in high school. They were good about my hours, so I was able to get off in time to pick up our daughter from kindergarten.

33

The Falls and the Bigger Falls

You would think Idaho Falls was named for its beautiful natural falls that cascade through the middle of town making for some picturesque views.

In a way, that is correct. It is named for the picturesque falls that help generate power as well as beauty. The falls, however, are not natural. They were fashioned with a drop of 20 feet over a width of about 1200 feet in order to generate hydroelectric power. The project was several projects, starting in about 1900 and going through about 1917.

Residents of former Taylor's Crossing, at that time, Eagle Rock, again re-named their town Idaho Falls, Idaho in 1891 after the beautiful natural rapids that graced the Snake River flowing through their town.

Over the years the beautiful falls have seen many natural changes due to time and the breaking of the Teton Dam in 1976. The city of Idaho Falls presently owns five hydroelectric plants on the Snake River.

Idaho Falls is the county seat of Bonneville County. It was named after explorer, Captain Benjamin L.E. Bonneville, who arrived on the Snake River plains in the

fall of 1832. He spent the winter around the area of
Menan, (about 15 miles north and west of present day
Idaho Falls. now a small country town with a population
of about 700 people.

The next spring, Captain Bonneville, working for the U.S.
Army, explored the Upper Snake River Valley and
adjacent Snake River plains.

It has been said that, although he was on leave of
absence from the army to explore the fur trade, that he
was actually under orders from the War Department to
explore the West, learning all he could about the area's
natural history, native inhabitants, geology, geography
and climate.

Bonneville's explorations were later published by
Washinton Irving, who noted in his later writings that
Bonneville considered the Craters of the Moon area,
(now a national historic monument south and west of
Idaho Falls about 87 miles on US 20/26), to be a desolate
wasteland with little redeeming qualities, "save its wild
and majestic nature".

An interesting fact about the Craters of the Moon is that
it is purported to be one of the youngest volcanic areas
in the state. It is also possibly one of the most likely
areas to erupt sometime in the next 1,000 years if it
keeps to its time schedule, which is about every 3,000

years! Some other young volcanoes in the state somewhat nearby are in the Shoshone lava fields.

If you want to see falls that really fall, you need to see for yourself the natural falls a few more miles downstream and a truly fascinating natural wonder. Shoshone Falls State Park is about 169 miles following I-84/86 further southwest of Idaho Falls on the Snake River, by Kimberly. It is a majestic horseshoe shaped sight, flowing down volcanic rock from a height of 212 feet. It is higher than the famous Niagara Falls by 45 feet.

34

A Little about Idaho Falls and the Area

One principle employer of Idaho Falls residents is the Idaho Engineering Laboratory. It employs over 4,000 individuals. During the time we lived in Idaho Falls, we enjoyed excellent schools, and a wonderful public library. Now it also has a historical museum that was founded in 2003 and an art museum.

Originally, the Atomic Energy Commission set up the National Reactor Testing Station in 1949 in the eastern Idaho desert to test and operate various nuclear reactors, fuel processing plants and support facilities. It was set in the desert with Arco to the West, Idaho Falls to the East, and Atomic City to the south.

In 1974, the operation and name of the area changed to the Idaho National Engineering Laboratory. The name was again changed to the Idaho National Engineering and Environmental Laboratory in 1997 then reflecting a new mission including environmental research. Once again, in 2005, the name of the laboratory changed to INL, now emphasizing the role of the laboratory as one of the United States' leading national laboratories, something our state can be proud of.

Idaho Falls is a beautiful town any time of the year, and

we truly enjoyed the time we spent there. We explored the beautiful Teton Valley, north and east of Idaho Falls, on weekends and camped in the forests above, fishing in the mountain streams. The dogs and the kids slept on top of each other in the camper, tired out from their busy adventures during the day.

About 25 miles west of Jackson Hole Wyoming near the Idaho, Wyoming border on U.S. 26 is Palisades Reservoir. Our retriever, Mandy, loved to swim in that reservoir. It was also great place for the family to swim and for Doug and I to water ski, but only for the young and brave of heart, for the waters, nestled between high peaks of the Snake River Mountain range and the Caribou Mountain range, are rather fresh even on the warmest days of summer.

Another favorite place for us to visit was Island Park, at the western entrance to Yellowstone National Park. It is about 73 miles north and east of Idaho Falls on I-15.

 To be honest, the years have eroded my memories to a quiet, serene place in mystic shadows of still waters shaded by large groves of trees. I remember crossing a little foot bridge over water clear enough to see fishes swimming just out of reach, running through sunny meadows . I also remember Johnny Sack cabin and a waterwheel at Big Springs, the headwaters of Henry's Fork of the Snake River. This is a place so beautiful, it has provided a dreamlike memory that becomes real when I "Google" the location.

I need to revisit this place. I would recommend it to any nature lover!

35

Boise Bound

In late November of 1979 we said good-by to southeastern Idaho and Idaho Falls and set a course back to Boise.

As hard as the move was from Fruitland, this move was easy. To begin with, interest rates dropped considerably. In October, we took a trip to Boise and found a home to purchase. We were excited. We found a three bedroom ranch style, pole fencing, and a small barn on an irrigated acre of ground. There was a large field behind that was available to rent for extra pasture. Behind the barn was a large old elm tree with the perfect tree house for the kids. The neighborhood was on the northwest side of Boise, just out of the city limits off State Street.

It was a rural neighborhood surrounded in small ranches on one to five acres, with larger places, 20 to 40 acres beyond to the foothills. It was the perfect place to raise children.

Doug's parents lived on the second bench in South Boise off Cole Road, only about twenty minutes away.

Albertson's grocery was only about a quarter mile east

at the intersection of State Street and Glenwood. It was on the south side of State Street. Today, Albertsons still is there, but on the north side of State Street. Where Northgate Shopping Center now stands, an old stables, called the 4x4 stables stood. In the field were chickens and a couple of donkeys.

The whole family was looking forward to the move. Doug was excited that he would be working out of the State Police headquarters as Planning and Statistics Officer. He felt he was well suited for the job and looked forward to the challenge and the change from patrolling the roads.

36

The Snowstorm

The first winter snowstorm of the year hit as the movers put the last items in the moving van on a frigid evening in late November.

We originally thought we would be leaving earlier in the day. As it was, darkness wasn't far away as we packed one cat, two dogs and two children into the cars. Doug would drive his patrol car and I would drive the family car. We had already driven Mr. Ed, our trusty Ford pickup over to Boise and left him at Doug's parent's house.

Doug couldn't transport the children in his car, but he did take the dogs. I got the children and an unhappy cat.

As we started out on the freeway, the wind was blowing like it wanted to blow us backward all the way to Wyoming!

The snow was coming down in huge flakes and beginning to pile up. To make matters worse, it is quite an interesting experience following a police car for 280 miles. Cars would come barreling past me only to break hard and cut quickly in front of me as soon as they saw the police car. I felt like stopping and making a sign for the back of my car that said "Police Car In Front of Me!"

We hadn't eaten and the kids were fussy. The cat kept yowling. No cell phones back then, so I just had to follow Doug's signals.

Twenty six miles south and west of Idaho Falls on I-15, we passed the town of Blackfoot, the county seat of Bingham County, and the "Potato Capitol of the World". I was hoping Doug might decide to pull over here to find a place to eat, but no such luck. We continued on into the quickly darkening evening. The snow was sticking to the wiper blades, so I turned the heater on full blast and turned up the music to drown out the kitty sounds. Thankfully, our daughter fell asleep. Our son was looking at a book with his flashlight.

Blackfoot was originally called Grove City because of the multitude of trees in the area. The name was later changed to Blackfoot for the Blackfoot River that runs past the town. The Blackfoot Indians were originally encountered in the area, hence the naming of the river by explorers. The Blackfoot tribesmen were a nomadic tribe of skilled hunters. They frequently visited the area on their travels. Many of their tribesmen ranged as far as the Great Plains. It is said that originally they got their name from explorers that first encountered them as they were walking across a recently burned area on the desert plains. Their feet were black from the ashes.

We passed a sign on I-15 noting the Fort Hall exit. That got me thinking, as always about the old days, the explorers and fur traders that first came to the area to trade with the first settlers, the Shoshone and Bannock tribes.

The original Fort Hall is said to have been considered the most important trading post in the Snake River Valley. It was made part of the Fort Hall Indian Reservation under the treaty of 1867, which included about 160 acres of surrounding land. Fort Hall was originally a fort built along the soon to be called "Oregon Trail" in 1834 as a fur trading post by Nathaniel Jarvis Wyeth.

Fort Hall, Idaho later grew up about 11 miles east of that site.

About twenty-five miles further down the road on I-15, we passed the quiet little town of Chubbuck.

Chubbuck, named after a railroad conductor, Earl Chubbuck, was originally called Chubbuck Beet Run. A lot of sugar beets were hauled out of the area by train for processing. The name was eventually shortened to Chubbuck Crossing, then becoming simply Chubbuck. Chubbuck is a friendly farming town of about 14,000. Today, it primarily serves as a bedroom community for Pocatello. Many university students find less expensive housing and a laid back atmosphere here.

We pulled over at a Holiday Inn 5 miles further down the road. I was happy that it also had a café attached. We were in Pocatello and decided to stay the night. There was an indoor swimming pool. I can still remember how warm and steamy it was inside against how bitterly cold it was outdoors. We hauled in the kids, two dogs, the cat and some canned goods from the trunk that might freeze, plus all of my house plants. We must have been an interesting sight!

The dogs and kitty were marvelous! They acted like they did this sort of thing all the time! I guess they just thought we were camping!

After dinner, we all went swimming, (well, not the dogs or cat).

I do remember that everyone slept like they were dead that night. In the morning, the storm was over, but the wind still whipped and the roads were really icy.

After breakfast, the kids wanted to know if we could stay another day and go swimming again. We told them we would come back again someday, but for now, we needed to get on the road.

We will never forget that hotel or Pocatello for the welcome break and friendly people we encountered on that cold winter night.

Pocatello was named after a Shoshone Indian Chief, Tondzaosha Pocatello, who settled with a band of around 400 Shoshone people at the Indian Reservation around Fort Hall in the 1870s. He was an advocate for better living conditions for the Shoshone-Bannock people.

Pocatello is a beautiful city that lies along the tree lined banks of the Portneuf River, a tributary of the Snake. Founded in 1889 it soon became known as the "Gateway to the Northwest" as settlers joined the Oregon Trail near Pocatello and followed it to Oregon. Today, the Oregon Trail still runs pretty much alongside I-84 as it makes its way to the coast. In places you can still see wagon ruts.

Pocatello has a population today of roughly 55,000 people, and is the county seat of Bannock County. It is known best for the fact that it is the home to Idaho State University, founded in 1901. Idaho State University is Idaho's designated lead institution in Idaho for health professions. It is also home to the Idaho Museum of Natural History, which is located on the university campus. This is a must see if you are ever in the area.

The cars still cut in front of me as we continued on toward Boise, but at least the windows were clear.

37

Almost Home

Every time one of the children would ask "How much further?" that day, I would say, "We're almost home!" I think I was trying to convince myself.

The City of American Falls says on its website today "Where the Sun Shines in Every Window". I don't remember the sun being out that day, but I did get a warm feeling as I passed by.

I knew a girl in my sophomore year of high school named Diane. Her father, I believe was an engineer for one of the mining companies in the Silver Valley where I grew up. She moved mid-term, but we wrote letters to each other until we graduated. She came to the Silver Valley, I believe, from Logan, Utah, and moved from the Valley to American Falls. I remember being curious about American Falls and talking to her about visiting one day, which never came. She was a good friend, however, and I will never forget her.

The settlement of American Falls was first founded in 1888. That city or what is left of it, is now a ghost town under the waters of American Falls Reservoir along with skeletons of mammals that walked the earth 75,000 years ago.

In 1925 the Bureau of Reclamation began moving the town of American Falls in order to use the town site for the site of a reservoir for the dam they were to build.

American Falls Dam was an expensive project. It involved moving over 300 residents, their homes, businesses, places of worship and schools. They also moved the railroad across the river, raising its level by 22 feet. The project of moving the town and building the dam ran from 1925 to 1927.

When the reservoir hits lower levels, an interesting landscape of the underwater ghost town can be seen.

Remains of a 75000-year-old mammoth were discovered in 2015. Since that time, other fossils and remains have been discovered.

In 1975, it was determined that the dam needed to be rebuilt. A new dam was built downstream. That project took until 1978.

Although the dam and reservoir are used primarily for flood control, irrigation, and recreation, it also produces over 92,000 kilowatts of electricity. The city of American Falls has about 4,400 residents. It is the county seat of Power County.

Rupert appeared off the freeway to the right after leaving I-86 and heading more directly west on I-84.

Rupert is truly farm country. The Magic Valley, virtually constituting Blaine, Camas, Cassia, Gooding, Jerome, Lincoln, Minidoka, and Twin Falls counties is agricultural country, famous for their harvests of potatoes, sugar beets, corn, alfalfa, and mint, plus many large dairy farms and meat packing plants. Food processing plants provide another section of the workforce with year round jobs. Rupert is the county seat for Minidoka County. Rupert is the largest city in the county with a population just over 5700.

About nine miles further southwest is the city of Burley. It has a comfortable population of a little over 10,000 citizens and is located in a relatively high, (a little over 4100 feet), picturesque but rocky desert. Burley is the county seat of Cassia County.

Burley is full of surprises. It may sit in a desert of blue-green sage with large wheeled sprinklers raining water on a multitude of crops in the summer, but if you like to ski in the winter, you will love Pomerelle Mountain Resort just 43 miles south. It is located below Mount Harrison in the Albion Mountains in the Minidoka Ranger District of the Sawtooth National Forest. It lies just 30 miles northeast of the Utah-Nevada-Idaho border. It is not a large ski area, but you're in for a wonderful experience with great snow at a resort well suited for family skiing. Annual snowfall is about 500 inches a season.

Twin Falls, Idaho has a spectacular entrance. It's called the Perrine Bridge and it sits like an eagle on a branch jutting out in a 1500 foot truss arch to sit 486 feet above the mighty Snake River.

Twin Falls is a city of over 51,000 people and is the county seat of Twin Falls County. It was created in 1904 and was named for a waterfall with twin falls which lies on the Snake River on the border of Jerome and Twin Falls counties, a few miles east of the city. Unfortunately, the second waterfall doesn't flow anymore.

Several interesting places to visit if you happen to be passing by are The Herrett Center for Arts and Science, which can be found on the main campus of the College of Southern Idaho in Twin Falls. It is an anthropological museum also including, natural history, astronomy, and art. The Faulkner Planetarium and the Centennial Observatory are also located on the premises.

Other must sees are Shoshone Park and Waterfall, (mentioned in an earlier chapter about falls on the Snake River), located approximately three miles east of the town; Perrine Coulee Falls; or if you're in for a short hike, Pillar Falls is on the Snake River upstream from Perrine Bridge and downstream from Shoshone Falls.

Natural basalt pillars take the river into multiple channels winding their way towards a roughly 20 foot drop.

You can even visit the site of Evil Knievel's attempted Snake River Canyon jump in September of 1974, located close to the visitor's center.

The day was starting to warm and the sun peeked through the clouds as we steamed past Jerome, beckoning us to stop for a break and lunch. No such luck, Doug never even braked.

The inviting and picturesque agricultural city of Jerome, the county seat of Jerome County, also beckoned to us as we drove by. The last census of 2020 reported its population at just over 12,000, making it the 19th largest city in Idaho.

The Minidoka Relocation Camp, one of ten such camps set up during World War II to intern Japanese Americans, was located in Jerome County. It sat about six miles north of the small community of Eden near another small community that no longer exists, called Hunt. Reminders of the camp can still be found in the desert today.

Twenty-one miles northeast of Jerome on ID-25 lies Wilson Butte Cave, listed on the national register of historic places. From a distance, it looks like just a large pile of dark colored basalt. When you come nearer, the pile of rock opens into a large cave entrance branching towards the northeast into two smaller tunnels. This important archaeological find was not discovered until 1958.

The news on the radio told me that on this day, November 1, in 1955, the first case of airline sabotage in the United States occurred when a man planted dynamite in his mother's suitcase. She was on US Airlines flight 629 to Longmont, Colorado. Thirty-nine passengers were killed and five crew members. Wow! That was pretty sobering to contemplate.

It went on to announce that in 1960 on November 1, President Kennedy first announced his plan to start the Peace Corps. I remember thinking it might be nice to serve in the Peace Corps one day. I decided to switch radio stations at that point and tuned in to Kenny Rogers singing the popular tune "You Decorated My Life."

Although I was unaware, at that moment on that day, November 1, 1979, our future little girl was fighting for her life with meningitis in a hospital in Nampa, Idaho.

We were on the road a little over two hours by the time and we were passing the next town, Wendell. Wendell is a community of about 2700. It is part of Gooding

County.

Gooding, Idaho, just eleven miles north is its neighbor is the county seat of Gooding County. The city of Gooding has a population of just over 3,500 and was named for a local sheep rancher Frank Gooding, who became mayor of Gooding and went on to become Idaho governor and a U.S. senator before his death in 1928.

I have to tell you an interesting story I found out about Wendell. To begin with, the town was named after the son of the surveyor that platted out the town, Wendel Speer Kuhn. It was laid out alongside the Oregon Short line Railroad in 1907 and dedicated in 1908. The railroad offered "Colonist Fares" on special immigrant cars. A family could book space in the cars for themselves and any livestock they were bringing, along with household effects, and ride the train to (as they advertised), "Wendell 'THE HUB', a town of opportunity". When the immigrants arrived, they were shown the real estate office, run by the railroad.

I knew we were nearing Doug's favorite place to eat in Bliss, just down the road. It was the east end of his patrol route when we lived in Mountain Home. There was a diner there that all of the law enforcement men loved to stop by. I figured that was where he was headed.

It was only about seventeen miles to Bliss. I laughed at the thought. If only! I assured two impatient children that we were going to get good stuff for lunch and they could have a chance to get some energy out helping me walk the dogs!

To keep the kids entertained, I told them about some places I wanted to take them in the future that were very close by, but was not going to happen on this trip!

There are some astounding caves just east of Gooding near the neighboring town of Shoshone. Both Mammoth Cave and Shoshone Ice Caves are easy to get to and a memorable adventure. Ask anyone in Shoshone how to get to the caves and they can help. It is a congenial town of about 1400 people.

The other fun place for families is in Hagerman. Hagerman, Idaho has some beautiful waterfalls and a hot springs. Miracle Hot Springs and Banbury Hot Springs, about 13 miles south of Hagerman are and always were great places for family fun and camping. In about 1994, Leo Ray, owner of Fish Breeders of Idaho, reusing hot springs water, decided to raise alligators. By 1995, according to the Lewiston Tribune, he owned one-hundred-ninety-five alligators in Idaho's so called "Gator Bowl".

We did make it back for the caves, the hot springs and

the alligators in the 1990s. Alligators can still be viewed near the hot springs (behind a fence!)

And then we were in Bliss! The kids launched themselves out of one car while the dogs piled out of the police car. We enjoyed a good romp and a much needed bathroom break for all, including the kitty.

Bliss, Idaho boasts a population of 304 citizens. It is also proud to be the 151st largest city in Idaho. I have encountered only good experiences in Bliss. These experiences have been on the way to or from somewhere. It is friendly, welcoming and just a step away from adventure whichever way you choose to travel. Bliss resides in Gooding County, of which the county seat is the neighboring city of Gooding to the northeast. So, if you choose to go in that direction, your path will lead you to the caves I told you of previously and underground adventures. If you choose to go straight north of Gooding, 12.5 miles, you can walk through the "City of Rocks" a very unique geological area, filled with strangely awesome rocks in all sorts of sizes and shapes, including natural arches you can walk under.

If you choose to go south of Bliss about 10 miles, you will find the Snake River and a visitor's center at Hagerman Fossil Beds National Monument. Hagerman Fossil Beds contains possibly the richest known deposit of Pliocene Age terrestrial fossils. Most of the fossils are of horses that roamed the area around three and a half million years ago. This is also the site of one of the longest sections of wagon ruts preserved from the Oregon Trail which runs through the area.

Of course, we just came from adventures east of Bliss, and west, well we shall see what adventures lie in that direction.

Lunch was the best! I still miss that café! We knew as we loaded back into the cars that the hardest part of the trip was over. We were on "home ground" now. It was familiar road full of memories the rest of the way to Boise.

About 21 minutes later, we were passing through the railroad town of Glenns Ferry, serenely placed along the winding Snake River.

Glenns Ferry is always a welcome cool shady spot in the middle of the summer. Today, however, it was a welcome break from the ceaseless wind. It drops down in the canyon a bit and the surrounding high plateaus give some shelter. The desert wind, can be cruel in the dead of winter, and have a cooling effect in the summer.

Glenns Ferry's beginnings are best explained in a section On November 1, 1870, the Idaho Tri Weekly Statesman reported that a new ferry was established on the Snake River just above the Three Islands and a little below King Hill on the Kelton Road. It was said that twenty miles of travel would be saved by going this route which they described as "excellent road. It went on to report that the Toano road from Humboldt Wells would also cross at the same ferry, which was described as the old emigrant route, and the only direct one to the railroad at that time.

Glenns Ferry is still a town to put on the list for a day trip or camping trip of relaxation, history delving and pleasure. It boasts great places to eat, the Glenns Ferry Opera Theatre, camping at Three Island Crossing State Park with Oregon Trail educational programs and the Elmore County Fairgrounds and Event Center.

Today, we chugged on by the town of Glenns Ferry as snowflakes began drifting down again.

Following the Snake another eight and a half miles down the road, we passed through the sleepy little community of Hammett. Hammett is an unincorporated community, but with its close neighbor, (the City of Glenns Ferry), they are on my list of "best to retire in places". They are close enough to big city shopping to make it not really "out in the toolies", yet far enough away not to have the traffic. If you want a little land, you can still possibly have it, but if you want neighbors, there is still a bit of a town where you can walk to eat out or get the basic necessities. Water is obtained from an irrigation company for most large acreages and in the summer you go to sleep with the drone of the "shick, shick, shicka" of sprinklers. It stays green in the summer thanks to the irrigation and the Snake River still snaking its way toward the Columbia and the ocean. The high plateaus surrounding the area help make southwestern scenes silhouetted in the evening sunsets.

A little over twenty minutes later the kids and cat were sleeping; I was listening to John Denver and "Rocky Mountain High" on the radio. That song came out the year our son was born. I couldn't believe he was already a second grader!

The snow stopped falling, but the wind picked up. We were just going past Mountain Home. We had completed a circle of sorts in our wanderings.

It was blowing in a westerly direction. Hopefully it would speed our trip to Boise!

Just under an hour later, we pulled in to Doug's parents' home in what was then southwest Boise, off South Cole road.

That was the longest trip I've ever taken!

38

A Capitol Move

Life was about to change for the four of us, our dog and our cat in many ways.

The furniture arrived the next morning at 9:00 a.m. We were anxiously awaiting, keys in hand. The children already found a large sand pile by the barn and were exploring the tree house.

I was excited in that attached to stalls in the middle of the barn, was a separate room that would work well for a chicken house on one side and a tack room that would work for storage of gardening tools on the other side. We had no plans for horses; just a few small farm animals like chickens, rabbits, ducks or maybe geese would be fine.

I was already making plans to turn some of the large gravel area behind the house into a large garden for berries and vegetables and maybe plant a few fruit trees. There was a nice two-run dog kennel with warm box houses for the dogs when they needed to be outside.

Everybody pitched in with the move. Our children were happy with their "big" rooms". It was a ranch style home with three bedrooms at one end of the house and one bath that was also accessible to the master bedroom.

The middle of the home presented a family room with a nice fireplace, a living room to the front, a kitchen on the far end of the family room and a laundry room. The garage was for two cars but oversized.

The dogs needed to be kenneled while we worked because, although the whole property was fenced, it was split rail and they could just walk through, except on the east side against a neighbor and partially on the west side against another neighbor.

We settled in comfortably, almost like the neighborhood was designed for us. The road in front of us was dirt and dead end. It was perfect for our daughter to start learning to ride her bicycle. Our son was quick to stretch his bounds to three section corners away (they were not actual city blocks yet). At that point, he would arrive at Caswell road where the irrigation ditch that fed the properties was larger and he could actually catch fish with a friend he met that was the same age. His friend lived close to where they fished, and I worried more about occasional cars on the paved road than them coming to harm in the irrigation canal that was big enough to carry fish, but not big enough to carry away a child unless it was irrigation day. On those days, he was not allowed to fish.

We chose to put them in St. Mary's Catholic School since it was just down State Street and close to Doug's work and I was fortunate enough to land a job in the licensing section of the Idaho Motor Carrier Bureau, which was in the same complex. Things could not have worked out better.

39

Sick as the Dogs

Christmas Day 1979 found all us literally sicker than dogs! If it was a virus, it was wicked. It hit the kids first, then Doug and myself last. We experienced all of the classic symptoms.

Opening of presents was memorable. No shouts of joy and glee when our son got his train set and our daughter got the doll she wanted. We were the same. Everyone tried to stay up long enough to talk to family on the phone. I have some sad pictures of a dazed child playing with his train set and a little girl still in her nightie and housecoat at 3:00 in the afternoon sitting and holding her doll.

We ate chicken soup or nothing at all and went to bed. We went back to work and school after a week, but that mystery flu haunted us for almost two weeks before we all felt normal. We decided it just made us stronger, for no one got sick again for a long time!

During the time we were ill, I got lazy about letting the dogs out for exercise. They were really good about running in the field behind the house that ran along State Street. There was a pretty good mixed barbed wire and field fencing that fenced off State Street in most spots, plus the irrigation canal ran along the fence, so they would have to cross it. The neighbors had field fence on the back part of their yard where they had poultry, and the dogs had great recall. State Street almost 50 years ago was not the same road it is today. It was two lane country traffic bordering corn fields and pastures.

Sometimes I would go back in the warm house before the dogs got back for a moment to warm up. They were never left out alone for more than about ten minutes. Ten minutes is enough time to get in trouble.

One afternoon right after Christmas Mandy, our yellow Labrador came back with her tail dragging, and I mean literally dragging, and acting very strange.

I talked to her while I checked her out for injuries and found none, yet clearly, something was not right. I put her up in her kennel and thought maybe everything would be alright after she rested.

The next time I took her out, I walked with her around. The horrible truth was revealed. She had a broken spine back by her tail area. The only way she could go big bathroom was to run and it would fall out. She was x-rayed at the vet and found it was irreversible, but he thought possibly the feeling and use might come back if it was a blunt force injury, such as if she was hit by a car on State Street.

That was the only thing I could think that happened. She must have chased a cat and run out on State Street and got grazed by a car. We waited. Her condition never changed and she gradually lost weight. We had no choice but to put her down. I was heartbroken and felt extremely guilty. I never should have left her out on her own!

I carried that guilt for about nine months before Jessie turned up one evening crying out in pain. I had kept her close, but she went out in the pasture with me or the kids often.

We rushed her to the emergency clinic. They x-rayed and found a bb pellet lodged in her chest. It had just missed any vital organs by millimeters. She eventually healed and suffered no ill effects, but we both spent a few sleepless nights while she healed.

I questioned our neighbor who admitted casually to me that he shot her with a pumped up air rifle because according to him, "She got too close to my fence!" I asked him about Mandy. He admitted that she too had been the recipient of one of his bbs.

The dogs had been where they were supposed to be, in our pasture on our land. They had wandered close to the fence that bordered our land and our neighbor's. He had an additional fence up against ours with wire they couldn't get through. His poultry were safe, but I suppose they were sniffing along the edge on our side.

 We added a chain linked part which enclosed the yard area but left the pasture close to the neighbors off limits to the Jessie unless we were with her.

40

Boise and the Treasure Valley

When we were first married, in 1970, the population of Boise City was about 75,000. When we moved to Boise in 1979, the population had grown to a little over 100,000. Today, 2020, the population is being reported as 234,976.

The Boise Metropolitan area (the Treasure Valley, including six counties, Elmore, Ada, Gem, Owyhee, Canyon, and Payette), (opinions vary as to the exact description of the Treasure Valley, some sources leave out Elmore, or Owyhee counties, but I found the National Weather Service broke the Treasure Valley into two parts, Upper Treasure Valley and Lower Treasure Valley, including all six counties), have a combined population of over 700,000. It is the most populous metropolitan area in Idaho and contains the state's three largest cities: Boise, Nampa, and Meridian.

Although you can drive through all three of these cities and hardly feel you have left a big city, they each have their own distinctive flavors.

Boise has all of the old buildings and historical architecture, blended with the new. The capitol mall area is still an enchanting place to visit. I love to go into the tunnels that run under the capitol building to various government office buildings across the streets like the Law library, the Hall of Mirrors and the Len B. Jordan Building. There is also a restaurant where you can stop and have lunch.

Eighth Street Marketplace holds on to a piece of the past and is an intriguing area to visit, as is Harrison Boulevard. On Warm Springs Avenue, many of the large plantation-like homes are still heated by hot water that flows from warm springs.

The Old State Penitentiary and the Idaho Botanical Gardens next door, just up Warm Springs Avenue are two more tourist attractions that are worth the time. The Idaho State Penitentiary first opened its doors in 1872, while Idaho was still the Idaho Territory.

Interestingly, the first person to hang for murder in November 1901, after Idaho became a state, was a man from my hometown of Wallace.

Edward Rice's hanging haunts me. After research into his demise, I found that had he been tried today, or if he had been allowed the change of venue he requested, he probably never would have been convicted. He was accused of murdering a cigar store owner. The evidence was all circumstantial, and thin at best. To the day he was hanged, Ed Rice maintained his innocence.

The Boise City Zoo, the Discovery Center, and the paddle boats in the City Park along with hiking or biking the greenbelt and floating the Boise River are also some "must do's" when visiting Boise, The City of Trees.

Meridian, though it is growing by leaps and bounds and includes one of the most popular new malls, complete with ice rink and dine-in movie theatre, still retains some of that friendly, country farm appeal in its downtown streets.

Nampa is quickly changing from total farm town to a city on the go with probably one of the larger out-of-state population increases due to less expensive homes swallowing up once fertile farm land.

All of these cities in the Treasure Valley have amazing parks.

41

The Family Grew

I wanted our children to experience a small piece of farm life if it was possible. It wasn't long before we added chickens, rabbits and a pair of geese to our little spread.

Our daughter still had a slight milk allergy and I found in Fruitland that she thrived on goat's milk. I decided to get a milk goat or two. It wasn't long before the refrigerator had too much goat's milk on its shelves. I didn't have as much time to do all the baking I did in Fruitland since I was also working. We decided to get a couple of calves from the auction.

Off to the auction we went in our little Toyota fastback. I don't know what we were thinking!

An old Herford came in to the ring with twin calves trailing. Her udder was half black. One calf was bawling while the other had to be carried to the auction ring. The twin calves were born the night before in the yards. The mother cow turned in the ring revealing a swollen milk bag with one half of it shriveled and blackish in color.

We got the bid and became the owner of twin Herford

female calves. An old timer walked up to us and said we had a deal if we could keep them alive because if they were one of each sex, they were probably sterile, but since they were both girls they probably weren't. I still don't know about that.

We spread a tarp and put them both in the back of the Toyota with the seats folded down. The kids rode with them.

When we got them home, I loaded them up with penicillin, put heat lamps on them and proceeded to ply them with goat's milk.

It was slow going. Neither would suckle. The one that was full of energy finally took off and started eating. It was all I could do to put my fingers in the other's mouth and gently drip the milk along my fingers and get it to pour into her mouth. She got small bits down, but at least some. I did this every hour then every two hours as she got more.

I was up and down all night. By morning the one we named Nellie Belle, the one that was half dead, was standing and bawling for more food. The one that was full of energy and drinking the day before was sick and passed away before the day was done. Those girls were the first bummers we ever started, but they certainly weren't the last.

Nellie Belle became the family pet. She followed us everywhere and generally was easy going unless startled. They she would kick up her heels and take off like a bee stung her! I never had the heart to sell the females for "canners", so the only other two calves that stayed around past "canner" stage were Brownie, (another Herford calf that looked like a stuffed toy when Doug and our neighbor came home from the auction one day with Brownie stuffed behind the seat of an El Camino), and Candy Calf, (a Holstein calf that was also born in the auction yards).

We rented the pasture that bordered State Street, where storage sheds now reside. We had irrigation privileges with the rental agreement, so the grass grew late into the fall and early in the spring.

The only scary issue was that at times, stray dogs would get out in the pasture to chase the animals. Once it happened while I was at work. I received a call from our neighbor that our two horses and three calves were out in the middle of State Street!

Luckily, I did not work far from home, just over off Chinden Boulevard. I rushed home and found all five of them eating along the side of the busy road. They followed my lead and all went back across the ditch and home as soon as I told them it was dinner time!

I was never so relieved! Imagine what it would be like with the traffic on State Street today if horses and cows were wandering around amongst the traffic!

42

If Life's going Well, Complicate it a Bit

Life was going along at a nice pace. The children were doing well in St. Mary's School. We became members of the Parrish and looked forward to our weekly visits, and after-church activities.

At home, we added chickens, a pair of geese, some rabbits, a pony for the kids and a little Tennessee Walker/ Quarter Horse mix mare for me that I watched grazing in the pasture behind our house for many months. I called the owner one day and asked if she was for sale and if she was broke. Five hundred dollars and a test ride later, she was my horse!

I loved riding bareback on my little mare, down the road, with the kids following behind on their pony. I found that a neighbor lady that owned a team of Appaloosa horses. They pulled a wagon in the summer and sleigh in the winter time. She also did her own horseshoeing. Bernie would trim and shoe my mare for a really decent price.

A skilled horsewoman, she became a great riding partner. In the years that followed, this lady, Bernie Jestrabeck-Hart, became well known for welding awesome metal art out of old fence wire. One of my favorites, "Three Deer" stands in Ann Morrison Park in Boise.

One spring afternoon just before Easter in 1982, the phone rang at my office desk.

Since I began working at the Motor Carrier Bureau in the fall of 1979, I was promoted to Supervisor over the IRP (Interstate Registration Program) and Pro-rate Interstate and Intrastate Registration Program for Idaho. I loved the job and the team that I worked with. It was both challenging and interesting and I met a lot of interesting people. I also admired and respected both of my supervisors, Gerald "Jerry" Sander and Shirley Reich.

I was surprised to find the caller was from the Department of Health and Welfare, the adoption section. Doug and I and the children decided the year before to go through the rigorous process of applying to adopt. The process was long and drawn out. By the time we were done, we felt it was much easier to just bear children.

Since the loss of our first daughter, Julee, we both felt there was a vacant spot looking to be filled. We did not want to replace her, but we felt we possessed enough love left over that we should share it with someone else.

The first thing we needed to do was to put the questions

and shadows left from the loss of our first child to rest. Back in 1971, we received the results of the autopsy from the doctor that attended me during her birth. His answer was simply that she had "multiple problems as do many first babies" and died of a heart attack a little over two hours later. It was also mentioned that the area around her umbilical cord did not close right, but no detail was given. As time went on we watched our second daughter grow and excel in school, we started questioning what "multiple problems" was. It seemed the information he told us about the autopsy was a little vague. We never were given anything to read. I also remembered a doctor from the transport from NICU also told us that our second daughter "most likely had Down Syndrome". This was later proven wrong once they ran tests.

We called the Department of Health and Welfare and asked questions. They soon called us to a meeting where they read the actual results of the autopsy. Julee was born with an omphalocile of the exact size (the size of a quarter) of our second daughter's. She was found to have no other defects. The area of the omphalocile (in this case, the size of a quarter) needed to be immediately covered with a moist sterile dressing to keep the tissues from drying out. If the tissues dry out, (which takes about two hours), they will burst. The child was also born early, which we already knew. We were told all information in careful, kind words. It took many minutes for the gravity of this to sink in. I don't know if our minds even took it all in then.

We decided two things in the next few days. The first thing is that finally a lot of overdue unanswered questions were answered, and for that, we were appreciative of the Department of Health and Welfare. The second thing is that we could not bring back our child. All life is fragile. The life of a newborn is especially so. We already lived through so much in such a short time. We needed to focus on going forward with our children, while keeping Julee close in our memories. I remember clearly seeing my baby quickly wrapped in a receiving blanket, shoved into an incubator and wheeled off. This report brought back some disturbing gossip I heard after Julee's passing from the daughter of a hospital janitor. She had no idea she might have been talking about my child. Those things still haunt me, but I believe that Julee's life was short because she had better things to do in other places. She taught us much in that short life.

We began thinking about adopting a child from war-torn Vietnam. In the process, we discovered that right here in our Idaho State system there was an abundant supply of young children that were being passed over because they were not infants. Some experienced emotional or health problems. Many of these children were looking at being raised in institutions for the rest of their youth.

We did a turn-about and decided to adopt one or more "hard-to-place" children under school age. The "or more" came in if it was a sibling group. We felt we would not be taking an infant out of the arms of someone who had not been able to experience raising an infant, yet we could share our love with another child that might not get the chance of a family otherwise.

There was not a lot of education provided at that time preparing parents for what they might be opening themselves up for. One thing we stipulated was that we were not in for children that had been affected by drugs because we had no idea of what to look for or what to do, having no education or experience in that area.

The lady on the other end of the phone congratulated me and told me that our dreams were about to come true. We were to find ourselves the prospective parents of two beautiful children, a boy and a girl. The boy would turn five years old later that summer and the girl would turn three the month after that.

I was ecstatic! I couldn't wait to tell Doug and the children! The reaction of my co-workers was mixed. Two older ladies rolled their eyes. One took me aside and told me I had no idea what I was getting myself in to. She and her husband adopted a boy many years before. She attempted to tell me of their life of heartbreak. Her warning words fell on deaf ears. This was going to be different! We were going to be the saviors, we would fix all of their hurts and all would be well!

Many of the workers gathered around congratulating me. I was in heaven!

When I told Doug, he was also overjoyed. The kids were excited and wanted to know when they were going to meet their new little sister and brother. They wanted to go to the store and buy presents for them. They wanted to know all about them.

I told them everything the lady told me. A meeting was scheduled for that weekend. We would learn more then.

43

The First Day of the Rest of Our Lives

The first day we set our eyes upon our two younger children, is imprinted in my memory with indelible ink in color. They both stood behind a screen door of a 50ish style home in a town under 50 miles from where we lived.

This was a bit out of the ordinary for adoptions. Usually they place children (or used to) at the other ends of the state. This was especially true if it was a 'closed' adoption, which this was. The mother and fathers had already terminated their rights. They were the most beautiful children, one was as fair as the other dark, and both would melt anyone's heart. They had us heart and soul from the moment we set our eyes upon them.

They had their hands set against the screen, searching our faces for a sign of acceptance and recognition. The oldest asked, "Are you my mommy?"

The youngest had one thumb stuck in her mouth and looked up wonderingly with the bluest of eyes.

Our two children each approached them, our (now eldest) daughter with a cabbage patch doll for the little girl, our (now oldest) son with a basketball for the boy.

The little girl exclaimed with eyes full of joy, "Lookee Henee! We got rich!"

Everyone laughed, the tightness was gone. We all started talking at once. The case worker made introductions of the children and the foster parents.

I remember we ate lunch with them before big hugs and promises to see them again really soon. The little girl didn't want to let go of me. I still remember those grasping little chubby hands.

Things moved really fast after that.

We received a call from the case worker the next day. She would bring the children to stay permanently as foster children until the adoption process was completed. To our surprise, that would happen almost immediately! It was to be the Friday of the next week!

We were excited, but thrown in a panic. That would mean they would be home for Easter, which was the following Sunday. My brother, his wife and our little niece were coming for Easter Sunday. That was wonderful, but a lot to do fast.

We were going from 2 children to 4 children basically in a period of 2 weeks! We made a list of needed items. Pillows, blankets, beds! Toothbrushes, new clothes, age appropriate toys, chest of drawers for each to put their clothes in, the list went on.

I remember a trip to Fred Meyer where we loaded down two shopping carts. People must have thought we forgot when Christmas was!

We were fortunate in that some close friends from Mountain Home, who were raising four children of their own, and who now lived in Boise, were replacing their girl's beds. They gave us a nice set of bunk beds and a chest of drawers.

The boys were already set, since our (now older) boy already had a set of bunks in his room.

The day came and I can't remember being more excited. It even topped my wedding day. It was probably much more akin to the days I first held our other two children. I never held Julee.

Now, here is another indelible picture imprinted on my mind, in color. The caseworker was kneeling down beside our new little daughter and son on the front lawn. All of them are meeting our fourteen week old collie pup, purchased before our world so drastically changed.

Our two older children jumped right in to big brother and big sister rolls as soon as they got home from school. Our (now elder) daughter took little Krissy into their room they were to share to show her dolls and new toys, and our elder boy taking Henry out to the big sand pile to play with some new trucks.

Our life-changing adventure had begun. The way we would look at many things would be altered forever, and for the better. Things we took for granted, would not be taken that way anymore. We would learn, and learn to teach that there are things in life you need to learn how to live with, and that not everything can simply be fixed.

We would also learn that each individual is different, but different can be good and another chance to see things in another perspective.

We became firm believers that there is no answer as simple as "nature versus nurture". Nature can be curbed and nurture can help, but individual choice is the most important thing of all. Individual choice is affected by how a person views themselves. This is something that can be glued in a person's psyche very early in life.

All I can say is that we did the very best we could in the coming years, gave everything we could, and just loved. Life went on.

There were golden days, there were very frustrating days. One golden day I hold dear to my heart is a trip to the mountains we made that summer. On the way home, the kids all fell asleep. Back in those days, we didn't wear seatbelts, so I held Krissy on my lap. She fell asleep as the afternoon sun shone softly through the windshield glinting off her lightly colored hair. She was cuddled softly against me with her thumb stuck in her mouth. I remember at that moment thinking that I couldn't be happier. I was so thankful for the chance to love and care for all of my children and to have a loving and supporting husband.

44

A Home Maker

In July of that same year, 1982, Doug was offered a new job as head of the Ports of Entry for the Idaho Transportation Department.

This was a bit of a change, in that he no longer wore a uniform to work, or carried a gun, or drove a police car.

The Idaho Port of Entry System had just become part of the Idaho Transportation Department, whereas it previously was part of the Idaho State Police. He would also have to travel at times.

I was thankful for his new job because it became apparent by the fall of that year that it was not practical for me to continue my job at the Motor Carrier Bureau.

It would be hard for me to care for the children, and work when Doug was traveling plus it was becoming apparent that the two younger children needed more than daycare could give them. The youngest was the greatest worry. It was reported that she spent most of her days sitting in a corner. I was surprised, because when at home, she interacted well with the children and loved to listen to stories.

I figured out that it was easier to go back to basics and

re-potty train her. This was coming along nicely with the little potty chair we purchased her. We also discovered that her skills such as sitting in a swing, or climbing little slopes were severely behind. The caseworker explained that much of her life before coming into the system was spent in a crib.

She had just turned three and I felt she needed more time than just evenings and weekends devoted to her. I also felt our new son, who was anxious to join in with play, was also masking a lot of emotions including feelings of self worth and knowing just where he actually fit in the scheme of things. He seemed a bit pre-occupied by the latter. When my sister and her two children came down to visit and took a trip in to go to the park and zoo, he sat in the back seat between his sister and a cousin.

He looked at me and said, "Now, am I not number three anymore?   Am I number five?"

I gasped, realizing that it was possibly traumatic for him to go from #1 to #3 (oldest to third oldest in a family). Now, he thought his cousins would be joining "the family unit" and he would be down the line further in age, becoming only #5. I had a long talk with him, impressing the fact that where he was in age was not important, that all four children were #1, and that the cousins were only "visiting".

I turned in my notice at work in September and became a full time mother. Not for long.

School started and our neighbors were school teachers. They had two older daughters and a younger son, Tyler. Tyler was a joy. He was the same age as Henry and they played well together. They also shared and played with Krissy.

When I was offered the chance to take care of him and another neighbor's son who was the same age, I jumped at the chance. It wasn't easy going from a double income with twice the children. This helped immensely! I also thoroughly enjoyed the extra children.

As Krissy became more mobile, she ran everywhere. Her energy was endless. I loved to see that, but the worry was around the horses. No amount of warning could get her to slow down around them. She would zoom past their hind ends with nary a thought. After Krissy had a close call with my mare, and Henry almost got run down by stampeding cows after wanting to play "cowboy" with them, I decided the best answer was to find a new home for the horses and the cows. We could use the money, anyway.

The older children had outgrown the pony and it was apparent the younger ones weren't quite ready. Larger animals might be a thing we could think about again later, but now just wasn't the time.

That task was done in about two days. I already knew of a neighbor that offered to purchase my mare for his teen-age daughter if I was ever in the mind to sell. She went to a great home and we got to see her every day! The pony also went to a good family that lived close.

Another neighbor of ours wanted to purchase Nellie Belle so he could fulfill a dream of raising beefalo. Nellie was super easy to handle. I knew the neighbors were really fond of her and this way she was still in the neighborhood.

I insisted upon breeding Candy Calf (who was also a cow by now), so she wouldn't get butchered. A nice family bought her for a family milk cow.

Brownie became what Brownie was meant to become. He fed us well for many months to come.

We fell into a nice routine. The years passed and before I knew it, Henry and the other two boys that I babysat, were in the second grade and Krissy was in kindergarten. By that time, the other boy, whose mother was also a teacher, was going home with his mother. I would pick up Krissy at half day kindergarten and the boys at the bus stop after school and keep Tyler until his parents or sisters got home.

Things would have been perfect, except for the fact that the children were all growing and needs were getting greater and money was getting tighter.

I scoured ads for ideas. The fall that Krissy started the first grade, I added a couple of jobs. One was part time at the school as an aid and playground assistant. I also picked up a weekend and evening job taking care of a Laundromat. That did the trick. We weren't so tight for money and I still could be home with the kids.

The children all flourished. Our rabbit numbers grew. I learned of rabbit shows and teamed up with a few of the young neighbor girls who raised rabbits to learn more about the different breeds of rabbits. We learned how to turn our rabbits into pedigreed rabbits and read about how to show rabbits. We found that we could earn money for our rabbits by showing them if we got good enough to win.

With the permission of their parents, I would load up my four children and three or four of the neighborhood children, and we would go to the Treasure Valley Rabbit Breeders shows. The children would join in showmanship contests. They were thrilled when they started actually winning ribbons. This encouraged them to study more. We worked on breeding our Satin rabbits with our son's favorite rabbit, a Californian, English Spot mix. The result looked just like the new favorite variety all the Satin raisers were working on being accepted, the Broken Satin. Our son practiced what he learned about keeping breeding records. By the time the broken satins were accepted for show at the National ARBA show in Colorado, two of his does placed in the finals.

I was approached by one of the club members that encouraged me to start a 4-H club. I got the information and was intrigued. This was a way for all of the children to learn about rabbits, yet it was something they could apply to so many things in life, such as responsibility, making reports, giving speeches and demonstrations (generally, statesmanship), self esteem, the list went on!

I was sold on 4-H! Before I knew it, we formed Northgate 4-H. Over the years, we became a force to be reckoned with! Assistant leader, Kathy Ourada was a super partner. She brought three of her children to the group which then totaled about thirteen members. They owned a ranch in the Boise foothills. It was an awesome place for Halloween parties!

I am still proud of every one of our 4-Hers. They all wanted to learn and worked hard. The children worked on projects from baking and science to all of the small animals including but not limited to rabbits, cavies, dogs and cats. We joined with two other 4-H groups for horses and goats. This was a rich and rewarding time in all of our lives.

Many of my children directly or indirectly applied their 4-H experience to their lives as adults. Several of them are teachers.

Thinking of each and every one of these children, now adults, parents, even grandparents of their own, brings tears to my eyes.

I was supervisor for the small animal showmanship tent for a few years. All of the club members pitched in on this project. As a senior project, one of our members was instrumental starting cat showmanship at the Western Idaho Fair.

Years later, after our children all graduated, we discontinued Northgate 4-H. I judged rabbits and poultry for several counties including Canyon, Valley, Gem and Benewah. We donated all of our kid's trophies gathering dust to different fairs for re-use.

As Krissy entered the third grade, it was time to go back to work full-time.

After getting, once again on the state hiring roster, I was fortunate enough to land a job with the Idaho Transportation Department, District Three. I absolutely loved this job. I worked with people that worked with machinery and materials that I was used to being around as a youth, such as large machinery, tractors, trucks, trailers, welders, and backhoes. The list went on.

I learned survey, and was put in charge of the district maintenance survey for accountability of aggregate stockpiles.

I learned about the different emulsions used for paving, keeping track of the supply on hand at the District Office and ordering more when needed. There is no longer a need to keep much of the supply of emulsions at the District Offices now, since most road jobs are now contracted out.

I assisted the District Maintenance Engineer by taking notes on road inspections. He loved to teach about engineering, and taught me many useful things about what it takes to keep roads from falling in to rivers, or slopes from falling onto roads. When he explained it, it all made sense. I think I could have been an engineer in another life. I still love the smell of fresh asphalt!

I also handled the radio traffic for the District maintenance men. I liked to say that I told 100 some men where to go every day!

When they came up with the system to monitor the temperature of the pavement on bridges to know when to spread ice-melt, they installed the first personal computer in the District in our office to remotely read the monitors. They put it in our office, since we would need to notify the foremen on the radio when to go out and spread the ice-melt.

I was excited to find out that I was going to be sent to school to learn how to operate the personal computer, and it would be my job to monitor the system!

It wasn't long before I was "hooked" on the idea of all the possibilities of what a personal computer could do or might do in the future.

45

Breaking in to the Teen Years

The next ten years were exciting, challenging and, yes, frustrating years.

The children were growing fast. We already remodeled part of the house, taking a piece out of the large living room to create a small room for the kids to use their first personal computer in.

We also remodeled the kitchen, making a small informal dining alcove in addition to the large table in the family room. Doug made new kitchen cabinets and we put in a garden window. We borrowed a piece out of the oversized garage and added second bathroom with shower.

The home had a nice closed in patio. We did a little more work on this, making it usable for play, especially for things like Lego building or for 4-H meetings.

 By the time our oldest was in the eighth grade and the next in the sixth, making another in the third, and the youngest in the first grade, we were ready to consider making a major change.

Their bedrooms that originally seemed so large were bursting at the seams with toys. They were arguing about whose space was whose. Our bedroom was just across the hall and by the main bathroom. Doug and I had very little privacy.

It's interesting how the ages of children make a huge difference on how space issues are viewed!

We didn't want to move, so explored adding on another floor. Adding on out the back wasn't feasible, since our septic tank was right out the back door. There was no room in the front. Either side also did not work.

We were disappointed to learn that the footings on the house would not support adding another floor. The only option was to move.

We began looking, half-heartedly. Our hunt continued until late into the fall. One day, we were out for a drive up Pierce Park Lane. We passed a stables and a beautiful home on a creek that tumbled down from out of the foothills. There was a "For Sale by Owner" sign on it.

It was unlikely we could afford it, but we stopped and talked to the owners anyway.

We both fell in love with the house and property.

The older couple were in a position where they wanted to step down in house size. The more we talked to them, the more we felt there was actually a chance we could make this work.

They visited our home and fell in love with it. It would suit their needs just fine, plus there was room for a pair of their horses.

In a little over a month, we were owners of a home with room for our family to grow, a creek and a pond. The boys loved the pond. The first thing they did was to build a raft.

We also became owners of a stable business. It was called Pierce Park Stables.

The stables came complete with clients, stall cleaning and horse feeding.

That Christmas the children also got horses from Santa. Children and horses became part of an adventure that continued for more than thirty years. Animals are a good way for children to learn about themselves and a good way to learn about communicating with others.

46

More Homes over the Years

We eventually made our way to a log home on the north side of Eagle in the Boise Foothills. It was a great location. We enjoyed memorable horse rides into the foothills, across ridges, through what was to become the town of Hidden Springs, up Cartwright Road and beyond. We saw rattlesnakes, jack rabbits and coyotes on our rides and raced thunderstorms home.

We acquired a very small herd of beef cattle, raised from calves, built and mended fences and stayed active in 4-H with horse, cat, dog, rabbit, goat, chicken and teen leader projects. The experiences we had and the memories we made as a family and as individuals will stay with us forever.

Our family was growing and changing. It was a unit breaking out as the children's individual personalities, dreams and desires began to evolve.

Every day, as your child grows, it becomes more of an independent being. You pray every day that you have made an impression, a positive difference, and have protected the child to the best of your abilities.

There is no manual that will ever tell you how to exactly

raise each human being, because we are each born an individual snowflake uniquely different from another with a will of our own. What affects one child in one way, might affect a sibling, even a twin in a totally different way.

We just do our very best.

Over 50 years, we have moved 35 times, built four homes, have owned twenty-two and have rented thirteen times for short intervals. We have lived in sixteen counties and two states.

We didn't set out to make moving an occupation, but somewhere along the line it did become somewhat of a pre-occupation.

More times than not, it filled a need to better some situation. I still look back with the love of a parent upon many of the places we built or remodeled. We never left a home without making it better in some way.

Some great adventure has come out of each of our moves. The early moves were at the request of employers, or to further our education. As time went on, our moves were more of a convenience for one reason or another.

Some of the things we have learned are that:

Home is not a piece of land or a house. Home is family.

You can posses land, but you do not own it either. It can always be taken away, by natural disasters, by eminent domain, by misfortune and lastly, by death.

Sometimes it works better to make your home fit your family rather than making your family fit your home.

It helps to be flexible and imaginative when raising a family, always remembering that anything is possible as long as you keep an open mind, keep the communication lines open and give those teens a lot of outdoor time!

The state of Idaho with its plethora of lakes to fish, mountains to hike, trails to bike, slopes to ski, paths to snowshoe, caves for spelunking, ghost towns to explore has been the best place to raise our family and enjoy our grandchildren.

 I hope you might also take the time to enjoy much of what Idaho has to offer.

Epilogue

I come to the end of my story three-hundred fifty some odd miles from our home in the Silver Valley. We are still in Idaho, back in the Payette River Basin, but have once more changed our address. Needs change, families grow and age. We have found the forests of the southern part of the state as welcoming and full of adventure as the ones we were born in. I miss the Valley, but love being closer to grandchildren.

Who knows what is in the future!

ABOUT THE AUTHOR

Author, Eloise Kraemer and her husband, Douglas were born and raised in Idaho. Her first book, "Across the Crooked Bridge" is a historical biography, tracing her life through the changes in the Silver Valley during that time period. She has since written "Idaho in Pictures and Poetry", which includes facts about different areas in Idaho; two teen books of the historical fiction genre, blending local history of the area with a fictional plot, and a children's story about animals living in the same Northern Idaho forests.

Eloise says she has been fortunate to have lived in almost all parts of this great state, and has come to love it all.

She and her husband currently live in the mountains near Boise, Idaho. They enjoy hiking, kayaking, photography and snowshoeing together with their three dogs, Sharlie, Orian and Brea. Eloise still gets in a ski trip or two with children and grandchildren each year.

Spending time with her grandchildren, photography, writing and gardening are her passions.